Accounting Classics Series

Publication of this Classic was made possible
by a grant from Arthur Andersen & Co.

Suggestions of titles to be included
in the Series are solicited and should
be addressed to the Editor.

Books in
The Accounting Classics Series
Editor: Robert R. Sterling

THE PHILOSOPHY

OF ACCOUNTS

by

CHARLES E. SPRAGUE, A.M., Ph.D., C.P.A.

Scholars Book Co.
Box 3344
Lawrence, Kansas 66044

ISBN: 0-914348-09-4
Library of Congress Card Catalog Number: 72-81869
Manufactured in the United States of America

Foreword to the Reissue

Some sixty years ago I happened to enroll in an accounting principles course at the University of Michigan. The instructor in charge was David Friday, a professor of economics who knew nothing about accounting. But Friday was an excellent teacher and understood the importance of keeping ahead of the class when embarked on strange waters. For some weeks our progress was slow, mainly because the book we were trying to use, *Accounting and Auditing*, a bulky volume printed by the Cree Publishing Co. of Chicago, was a confused presentation baffling to instructor as well as students. (I shall refrain from naming the author—a well-known professor who did some better writing later on.) Then one day our teacher came in beaming with two books of modest dimensions which he held up for us all to see and recommended strongly. One was *The Philosophy of Accounts* (1907) by Charles Ezra Sprague and the other was *Modern Accounting* (1909) by Henry Rand Hatfield. Professor Friday shortly had two copies of each of these books placed on reserve in the library, with use restricted to members of his class. In my case the availablity of Sprague and Hatfield in connection with this course was crucial. It was these writings that aroused my interest in accounting, and without this spur I am quite certain that I would never have shifted from teaching economic theory to a career primarily in the accounting field.

Colonel Sprague died in the spring of 1912, shortly before I became acquainted with his *Philosophy*, but I was so much impressed with his writings and illustrious career that I pushed hard for his posthumous election to the Accounting Hall of Fame when this roster was established by Ohio State University in 1950, and he was selected for this honor three years later. I like to think that my effort was a major factor in bringing about this result. The citation for Colonel Sprague stressed his participation in drafting the first CPA law in New York, his many services to the State Society, his decisive role as a founder of the School of Commerce, Accounts, and Finance of New York University, his presidency of the Union Dime Savings Bank and offices held in banking organizations, as well as his outstanding work as a writer and teacher. An officer of the bank he had headed was on hand to respond and accept.

Prior to the appearance of *The Philosophy of Accounts* in 1907 Colonel Sprague had published an outstanding work, *The Accountancy of Investment*, and some related materials including *Logarithms to 12 Places and Their Use in Interest Calculations* and *Extended Bond Tables*. In my judgment these earlier writings are superior on all counts to anything in this area that has been published since. Sprague was a stickler for accuracy and sound analysis. His discussion of bond contracts, and the nature and treatment of discount and premium, is logical, thoroughgoing, and a far cry from the absurd procedures which have continued to be dominant in accounting practice, in the tax field, and in most of the textbooks. That the reportable liability at date of issue is the sum invested by the bondholder, not the amount payable at maturity; that the "discount" if any is an element of the total interest, which should be accrued systematically over the life of the contract at the effective rate; and that the "premium" is the portion of the amount received by the borrower which is repayable in the guise of the periodic contractual "interest", and which should also be systematically computed—these are conclusions that cannot be avoided by anyone taking the trouble to study Sprague's *The Accountancy of Investment*, first published nearly seventy years ago. In the light of this early presentation of sound thinking and procedure, the handful of us who have continued to stand our ground with Sprague through the years cannot help finding the record of what accountants generally have been saying and doing both painful and discouraging. I should perhaps note that in 1914 Sprague's writings in this field were put together in a single volume by L. L. Perrine, with minor revisions, which was published by Ronald Press.

In appraising *The Philosophy of Accounts* sixty-five years after initial publication it is important to recognize that when this book appeared "there were, indeed, few American texts which could lay any claim to scientific distinction" (to quote from Hatfield's "Introductory Note" appearing in the 1922 edition, published by Ronald Press). Sprague brushed aside the tiresome, muddled, fanciful rules-of-thumb that had cluttered the texts on bookkeeping for many generations, and presented the framework of accounting procedure logically in terms of the basic financial components and concepts of the business entity, with respect to measurement of both position and performance. He ignored the weird practice of personifying accounts, one of the longstanding crutches supposed to be helpful in the process of deciding what and when to *debit* and what and when to *credit*. He likewise abandoned the prevailing absurd methods of account classification in favor of arrangement in terms of underlying business data and objectives. Above all, he pushed the door ajar to a realization that accounting constitutes the outstanding approach to a pervasive understanding of business enterprise, with its complex array of transactions and operations, and the continuing need——throughout—for financial measurement, reporting, and planning. Please note that in the name of the "School" which he aided mightily in founding the word "Accounts" appears. I wish that this term were included in the rubrics of our schools of business generally. Unfortunately, accounting is all but buried—and lost sight of—in many of these schools because of the choking growth of subject matter which I regard as largely weed trees and underbrush. And I believe Colonel Sprague would agree with me if he could view the current scene in business education.

I cannot forbear adding that if Sprague were here today I am confident he would deplore the rut into which the accounting profession has fallen in bending the knee to the view that the recorded dollars in the accounts, regardless of their dates, are the only data worthy of being reported, and are not to be disturbed, no matter what happens to prices and other market evidences of change, except for the purpose of depreciation or amortization as time passes. Sprague would never have endorsed such an unreasoning, stultifying posture.

Not having known Colonel Sprague in the flesh, I am handicapped when it comes to appraising his character and personality. A review of what we know of his career shows him to have been a man of great versatility. Born in 1842, he served with distinction in the Union forces in the Civil War and was seriously wounded at Gettysburg. In professional life, as already noted, he made notable contributions in educational development and teaching, in accounting and banking societies, and as a financial executive. His scholarship is reflected in his earned and honorary degrees and the quality of his writing, including his outstanding pioneer work in what is often referred to as the actuarial field. He was much interested in the problem of international communication, especially in commerce, and in 1888 prepared and published a *Handbook of Volapük*, designed to acquaint Americans with a synthetic universal language developed a decade earlier by J. M. Schleyer, a German cleric, and well-known in linguistic circles in Europe. He was a bit of a reformer in English spelling, but his use of "positiv" and "negativ" in the early printings of *The Philosophy of Accounts* scarcely warrants high praise.

The four friends of Colonel Sprague who provided "Introductory Notes" for the fifth edition of *The Philosophy of Accounts* present a revealing picture of his personality. "He was one of the finest men I ever knew . . . a gentleman of the old school, courtly, sensitive, tactful . . . a scholar without pride of attainment, but insistent . . . on scientific accuracy" wrote Dean Joseph French Johnson. "Man of affairs and of books, original in modes of thought, urbane in demeanor, cosmopolitan in interest, high type of the scholar in business" wrote Professor Hatfield in offering a personal tribute at the end of his appraisal of Colonel Sprague's writing. All four stress the Colonel's achievement as a teacher and his devotion to logical reasoning and analysis in both oral and written presentation.

It is a high privilege to have been given the opportunity by Professor Sterling to prepare a brief introduction to *The Philosophy of Accounts*, now being reprinted as a "Classic" in the field, but I realize, keenly, that my effort falls far short of doing justice to Colonel Sprague, and his ice-breaking contribution to accounting theory.

W. A. Paton

PREFACE

It is not within the province of this treatise to teach the Art of Bookkeeping. Skill in that art is attained by practice, either in recording actual transactions in the counting room or those, simulating actuality, which are prepared for practice in the school or in the many excellent manuals of instruction. But facility in the processes of an established system will not satisfy the inquiring mind of one who has gone thus far; he will desire at a proper stage of his development to know the scientific basis of all systems, the wherefore as well as the how. When the subject is taken up at the collegiate or university stage, it is especially fitting that the science of accounts be unfolded concurrently with thorough drill in the art which depends upon it.

As a branch of mathematical and classificatory science, the principles of accountancy may be determined by a priori reasoning, and do not depend upon the customs and traditions which surround the art. I have endeavored to set forth these principles simply and naturally without resorting to fictitious modes of presentation, but adhering to the fundamental equations and their subequations.

I hope that my work may be of some utility to the profession of public accountants in the training of their assistants, as, even in routine matters, the best work is done by those who understand the theory and the reason of what they are doing. To business managers who have not been practical bookkeepers, it may be that I may throw some light on the methods in use and perhaps point out where they may be made more effective.

I had at one time intended to extend the book by adding to the twenty-one chapters here given relating to Accounts in General, a Part II on Accounts in Particular, in which should be taken up all the principal forms of account with various suggestions as to handling them. I found, however, that the task would reach encyclopedic proportions if I treated each type of account with the degree of thoroughness which has been given to Cost Accounts by several authors and to Investment Accounts in my work on "The Accountancy of Investment." I have therefore contented myself with an Appendix, containing some Monographs on a few very essential accounts.

I am conscious that the work will deserve and receive severe scrutiny as it is the product of over thirty years' handling of accounts in all grades of service and of six years' teaching the subject in the School of Commerce, Accounts and Finance of New York University.

CHARLES E. SPRAGUE

54 West 32d Street, New York,
September, 1907.

CONTENTS

THE PHILOSOPHY
OF ACCOUNTS

CHAPTER I

NATURE OF THE ACCOUNT

What Is an Account?—Definition of an Account of Value—Increase and Decrease—An Informal Account—Introduction of Totals

1. The word "account," used in its broadest and loosest sense, means not merely a narration, or a statement of facts, but something systematic or orderly. A rambling tale narrated by a gossip would not be an account because it is not systematic. An account must be a systematic statement of facts; but this is not all, it must tend or point to some conclusion. An account, as distinguished from a mere narration, is intended to establish some conclusion, to prove or disprove some proposition, and its parts, the facts of which it is composed, must bear upon this conclusion and must either favor or oppose it. Hence these facts or elements of the account may either be all of one tendency or some of them may be of an opposite tendency to the others.

2. But the accounts of which we are trying to discover the philosophy are of one class; the original class which gave the name to all the others, namely, accounts of value or financial accounts, and for these we may, summing up the foregoing requirements, adopt as our definition:

An account is a systematic statement of financial facts of the same or opposite tendency leading to a conclusion.

3. As increase and decrease are the two opposing tendencies in financial facts, an account must in its form provide for discriminating between these tendencies, distinguishing increase from decrease, positives from negatives, + from −.

3

4. A very primitive, yet logical and effective, form for an account might be one in which space was reserved for only one column of figures and where a conclusion was reached after every entry, the distinction between increase and decrease being expressed in the text alongside.

Thus let it be supposed that I require to keep an account of my deposits with a certain bank. The conclusion sought for is, how much have I in the bank? The positive, or plus, or additive, or increase elements of the account are the moneys which I deposit; the negative, or minus, or subtractive, or decrease elements are the sums which I draw out. If, then, the facts were that I deposited $2,000 and also $500 and that I drew $300 and $600 successively and again deposited $1,000, an account might be constructed as follows:

FIGURE I

Deposited..........................	$2,000
Deposited..........................	500
	$2,500
Drew..............................	300
	$2,200
Drew..............................	600
	$1,600
Deposited..........................	1,000
	$2,600

5. This is certainly an account, and it accounts for the conclusion, which is that the amount now in bank is $2,600. It is not in the ordinary form of an account, it is not in the most effective form for many purposes, and it is lacking in details which give incidental information; yet it conforms to the essentials of an account and not only leads to a conclusion but expresses it.

6. Elaborated into an account giving greater information, yet retaining its simple form, this might read:

FIGURE 2

MY ACCOUNT WITH THE FIRST NATIONAL BANK

1906 Jan.	2	Opened my account by depositing check of William Jones for......................	$2,000
"	7	Deposited currency received from sale of cattle.	500
		Balance in bank.....................	$2,500
Feb.	1	Drew by check No. 1 to the order of John Smith for 6 months' interest at 6% on mortgage of $10,000...............................	300
		Balance in bank...................	$2,200
"	4	Drew by check No. 2 to the order of Peter Men-ken for a loan to him...................	600
		Balance in bank...................	$1,600
"	24	Deposited checks of William Jones..........	1,000
		Balance in bank...................	$2,600

7. Here we have given many details of the transactions which will serve to identify them and enable us to prove them if necessary, thus furnishing information and protection. As every transaction has a date and an amount, we have ruled vertical lines to contain those particulars. This is on the principle of tabulation, that is, of allotting a separate column to any series of related facts which occur with regularity.

8. Simple and unconventional as this method is, it is used in substance by many good bookkeepers on the back of the check stubs where they keep account of the bank balance by alternate additions and subtractions. Strange to say, these bookkeepers and some excellent accountants would be horrified to see a ledger account which was not adorned with a "Dr." and "Cr." over the top and with repetitions of the prepositions "To" and "By" on every line, thus doubly emphasizing the fact that the left-hand side *is* the left-hand side. They would defend the simplicity of the stub account by saying that it was *not* an account, which is a very easy, but not very satisfying, way of disposing of the difficulty.

We must insist, however, that the statement given above is in essence an account.

9. The principle of tabulation, or columnizing, may be applied to this account by providing two money columns instead of one, and in the additional column placing the subtractive entries.

FIGURE 3

FIRST NATIONAL BANK

In account with [Me]

Date			Deposits	Checks
1906 Jan.	2		$2,000	
"	7		500	
Feb.	1			$300
"	4			600
"	21		1,000	

We do not need to label the several entries as "Deposit" and "Check"; by allocating each to its proper column we indicate this more clearly, and we have the further advantage of readily ascertaining, even in a much more extensive example, the answers to these questions:

How much are the Total Deposits?
How much is the Total Drawn?

These are very valuable pieces of information, next in importance to the prime conclusion,

What is the Balance?

10. It is therefore the custom, and wisely so, to separate the positive and the negative elements and to sum each by itself.

There are occasional exceptions to this and rightly so if anything is to be gained thereby.

With this understanding, then, that the two tendencies are to be treated apart, we will next consider the form of the account.

CHAPTER II

FORM OF THE ACCOUNT

11. We will now consider what arrangement of space is best suited to the purposes of the account, the positive and the negative elements to be kept separate so that each may be totaled when desired.

12. The information which is required is the following: How Much Value? How? When? Why? and With Whom? as to each transaction. Supposing we are at present providing for one kind or tendency only, it is evident that the figures representing the amounts involved should be free and clear of the context which explains them and that there is no better method of exhibiting these figures than to place them in a vertical column. As they are frequently the result of a calculation embodied in the context, it is appropriate that they should follow the context and this brings the *money column* to the right of the text.

13. As the date when the transaction took place is the identifying clue which we use in looking for information, it should also have a free and clear space, allowing the eye to pass rapidly from one date to another, and this space should not interfere or be confused with the other explanatory matter; hence it will be advantageous to place the date column on the left.

The remaining explanatory text will occupy the central space and will seldom need subdivision. Its various details, With Whom, Why, and How, should, however, follow a uniform and unvarying order of sequence to facilitate reference. (Figure 4.)

8

FIGURE 4

[Date]	[Specification]		$	c
When	How	Why	With Whom	How Much

14. This is a frame into which may be fitted all items of the same kind or tendency; we have next to provide for those of the opposite tendency. The most obvious way of doing this is by repeating or duplicating the whole of the above scheme. This was anciently done on two pages but it is now customary, and generally more convenient, to use but one. (Figure 5.)

FIGURE 5

THE STANDARD FORM OF ACCOUNT

Date			$	Date			$
		a				a	

The narrow columns at the left of the money columns marked *a* are for the purpose of indicating in some brief way the exact source of, or authority for, the entries.

15. This standard, or traditional, form of the account is used in almost every set of books. There is no law, however, requiring it to be used and there is no harm in deviating from it when anything is to be gained thereby.

16. There is one feature in the standard form which should be noticed. There being separate date columns on the two sides, it does not present a chronological view of all the transactions. If this is desirable it can be attained by adding merely another money column to the form in Figure 4, interweaving the dates and specifications of both columns and separating the amounts only. This is often called the "journal" form, from the book of that name. (Figure 6.)

FIGURE 6

ACCOUNT IN JOURNAL FORM

[Dates in order of time.]				$		$	

17. A variation of this form provides a third column in which may be entered the balance, or resultant, of the two other columns, as at *c*. (Figure 7.)

FIGURE 7

THREE-COLUMN BALANCE FORM

			$		$		$	
			a		b		c	

18. These are the principal variants, but minor variations occur from the exigencies of certain businesses. For example, if it is very desirable to compare the corresponding amounts on the two sides the standard form may be changed so as to bring the two money columns together. (Figure 8.)

FIGURE 8

MONEY COLUMNS BETWEEN

Date		$		$		Date

In this example the money columns are not exactly in the center, on the supposition that the right-hand entries require briefer specification than those on the left hand.

19. The form of the account is a matter of convenience, rather than of prescription. While custom should not be deviated from without cause, it has no claim superior to utility.

CHAPTER III

CONSTRUCTION OF THE ACCOUNT

CASH ACCOUNT AS MODEL—MEANING OF EACH SIDE—EXEMPLIFICA-
TION—RESULTANT—EQUATION OF THE CASH ACCOUNT WITHOUT
NEGATIVE QUANTITIES—ACCOUNTS OF INDEBTEDNESS—ACCOUNT
OF "ME"

20. We have now given to the account a frame or mold to hold its contents; we must next consider what is to be placed in the frame and how arranged.

21. An account representing some form of wealth or property will be the simplest to begin with, and we select money because it is the easiest form of wealth to value. Such an account representing money (or any of the substitutes for money) is called a "cash" account from an Italian word meaning "box"; it is the money-box account.

22. Recurring to the definition of an account, we ask: What are the facts of opposing tendencies to be recorded in a cash account? Evidently increase and decrease of the stock of money in possession. What is the conclusion? The amount of that stock of money at the time of inquiry.

23. The facts may be designated by many pairs of names, as:

POSITIVES	NEGATIVES
Receipts	Payments
Into the box	Out of the box
Plus	Minus
More	Less
Increase	Decrease

The conclusion is known as:

POSITIVE

Stock of cash
Cash on hand
Cash balance
Balance

24. Let the following be the facts which it is desired to record, constituting the "items" of the account.

1. Having no money, I borrowed from A B $100 on January 1.
2. Received my salary on January 31, $50.
3. February 2, I repaid to A B $75.
4. On the same day I paid expenses $49.
5. On February 15, I loaned to C D $35.
6. Received my salary, $50, February 28.
7. Repaid to A B on March 3, $13.
8. March 5, loaned to C D $12.
9. Received salary on March 31, $50.
10. Collected on April 10 from C D $10.
11. Paid various expenses on April 14, $27.
12. Collected from C D on April 15, $20.

25. Using the standard form of account (Figure 5) and deciding arbitrarily that the positive or receipt items shall occupy the left-hand portion, we record the facts as follows:

FIGURE 9

CASH ACCOUNT

19—				19—			
Jan.	1	Borrowed from A B.........	$100	Feb.	2	Repaid to A B...	$75
"	31	Rec'd Salary....	50	"	"	Paid Expense...	49
Feb.	28	Rec'd Salary....	50	"	15	Loaned to C D..	35
Mar.	31	Rec'd Salary....	50	Mar.	3	Repaid to A B...	13
Apr.	10	Collected from C D.........	10	"	5	Loaned to C D..	12
"	15	Collected from C D.........	20	Apr.	14	Paid Expense....	27

26. We have now complied with the definition of an account in so far that we have made a systematic statement of these twelve financial facts, six of which are of like tendency and six of the opposite tendency. As the total of the receipts is $280 and the total of the payments $211, it is evident that the balance is, at the beginning of April 16, $69, which is the conclusion sought.

27. The account in its present form is a current account. It follows the course of time and gives a history of the cash. The conclusion, or resultant of all the facts, is necessarily made up at some certain moment, and, for reasons which will appear later, the same moment is usually chosen for recording all these resultants in a group of accounts.

FIGURE 10

CASH ACCOUNT

	$100		$75
	50		49
	50		35
	50		13
	10		12
	20		27
	$280		$211
Balance.........$ 69			

28. The most obvious way of recording the resultant, or balance, would be to sum up each side and set down the result under the greater sum, as shown in Figure 10. As we are now concerned with values only we omit the words.

29. This, however, is not the most usual way of expressing a resultant. The double lines drawn under both sides usually denote equality, like the sign =, and if they are not equal they must be equalized. The amount necessary to equalize the two sides of this account is the balance, $69, which we have inserted in italics (suggesting the use of red ink) to designate something which is not a current transaction but an instantaneous result, not an occurrence but an inference.

FIGURE 11

CASH ACCOUNT

$100			$75
50			49
50			35
50			13
10			12
20			27
			$211
		Balance........	69
$280			$280

Here is a true equation. All the receipts exactly equal all the payments plus the balance. The preponderance of receipts is added to the opposite side to make equality, just as, in weighing butter, if the scales are out of balance, you do not take off some butter but you add on a weight.

30. In mathematics the normal way of asserting a truth is by means of an equation. The account in its current form (Figure 9) merely gave the facts; it now asserts the conclusion. As subtraction in accounts (see Figure 1) may lead to confusion, the same effect is produced by *adding* to the other side.

$$280 - 211 = 69$$

is transposed to read:

$$280 = 211 + 69$$

31. This principle of compensation, or adding to the weaker side so as to produce equality, is a very important one in accounts, as will be seen when we come to treat of proprietary accounts.

32. The equation of the Cash account may be read in several ways:

Receipts = Payments + *Cash on hand*
280   = 211 + 69
In   = Out + *Remainder*

33. In this last form any account representing a property may be read.   The increase, by acquirement or otherwise, is recorded on the left-hand side; on the right-hand side are two things quite at variance, in fact, antagonistic; one the decrease of property or of value, the other the resultant or value in possession.

34. Taking the right-hand side of the above equations, we see that the two terms are contrary:

> 211 is what has been paid out.
> 69 is what has *not* been paid out.
> ———
> 280 is all that has come in.

Yet the 211 and the 69 are both on the same side.   It is necessary to discriminate carefully between these two kinds of terms and not to assume that because they are on the same side, they must be congruous.

35. To illustrate another class of accounts, those representing indebtedness, let us select from the twelve items in Figure 9, some which imply indebtedness.   Such are Nos. 1, 3, 5, 7, 8, 10, and 12.   Nos. 1, 3, and 7 relate to the dealings with A B, to whom the subject of the narrative becomes indebted and discharges the debt.   Nos. 5, 8, 10, and 12 represent the converse relation with C D, who borrows and repays.   As this loan to C D is very similar

FIGURE 12

ACCOUNT OF THE INDEBTEDNESS OF C D TO ME

| Feb. 15 | Loaned him.... | $35 | Apr. 10 | Collected...... | $10 |
| Mar. 5 | Loaned him.... | 12 | "   15 | Collected...... | 20 |

to a piece of property, we will place the positive elements, the moneys loaned, on the left-hand side and the repayments on the right.   (Figure 12.)   Notice that this is exactly the opposite side to the one on which each transaction is found in the Cash account. This phase will reappear hereafter.

36. C D is called our "debtor," and we are his "creditor." When he discharges the debt in whole or in part he is also called "creditor," by an extension of language; really he does not become creditor, but merely extinguishes debt. Hence we can make a useful shortening of the heading by merely writing the name of the debtor with the abbreviations Dr. and Cr. With this change the balanced account appears as follows:

FIGURE 13

Dr.			C	D		Cr.
Feb. 15	Loaned him....	$35	Apr. 10	Collected......		$10
Mar. 5	Loaned him....	12	" 15	Collected......		20
			" 16	*Balance*........		*17*
		$47				$47

Again we have the equation:

Indebtedness Incurred = Discharge of Indebtedness
+ *Balance Owing* or
Present Debt

or again:

Indebtedness Incurred = Indebtedness Discharged
+ Indebtedness *not* Discharged

37. The separate items on the two sides are called "debits" and "credits"; hence we have another form of the equation:

Total Debits = Total Credits + *Net Debt*

38. These words "debit" and "credit" are often applied by analogy to accounts where there is no idea of indebtedness, all entries on the left side being called "debits" and all on the right "credits."

39. The transactions with A B are the opposite of those with C D; the subject gets in debt to A B and gets out again. As in-

2

debtedness *to* us is entered on the debit side, it would seem that indebtedness *by* us should appear on the credit side, and as A B is truly a creditor, this is quite correct. Discharges of his claim are treated also as debits and thus we can use the same form as in the account of C D, the difference being that C D's account has the larger total on the credit side and the balance on the debit.

FIGURE 14

Dr.			A	B			Cr.
Feb.	2	Repaid him.....	$75	Jan. 1	Loaned by him..	$100
Mar.	3	Repaid him.....	13			
Apr. 16		*Balance*........	*12*			
			$100			$100

40. As another way of looking at accounts of personal indebtedness it may be noted that in both accounts, A B's and C D's, the left or debit side is *unfavorable* to the person named in the heading and the right side is *favorable*, so that instead of:

Debtor   and   Creditor

we might have entitled the sides:

Against   and   For
Adverse   and   Favorable
To the Bad   and   To the Good

41. These terms refer to A B and C D respectively and to any other debtors and creditors. But as regards the proprietor of the Cash account these terms must be reversed and what is favorable to the person with whom he deals is unfavorable to the proprietor and vice versa. So that he would be entitled to write:

Against Him   For Him
[but for Me]   [but against Me]

42. In the case of Cash, which is inanimate and cannot owe nor be owed, he can still designate the two sides as:

[For Me]   [Against Me]

43. Seven of the original transactions have now been doubly entered, once in the Cash account and once in some other account; each being in one place "for me" (debits) and in another place "against me" (credits). As the effect upon "Me" is neutralized in each pair, it is unnecessary to keep any account with "Me," as far as they are concerned.

44. But there are five remaining entries which appear to concern "Me" alone: Nos. 2, 4, 6, 9, and 11. We may open an account with "Me" and, following the precedent already established, place these five transactions each on the opposite side to where they appear in Cash account. "My" account may be headed "Against" and "For" just as if "I" were a stranger. We shall see by trial how this will turn out.

FIGURE 15

AGAINST			ME			FOR
Feb. 2	Expense.......	$49	Jan. 31	Salary.........	$50
Apr. 14	Expense.......	27	Feb. 28	Salary.........	50
Apr. 16	*Balance........*	74	Mar. 31	Salary.........	50
		$150				$150

45. "My" account shows a balance of $74 of preponderance in favor.

This balance is different from that of any of the other accounts. It does not represent property, nor indebtedness, but proprietorship. It shows the increase in wealth caused by income being greater than outlay, which has resulted in a present status of $74 net worth.

46. This is strikingly corroborated by an independent operation. Extracting the balances of all the other accounts, we make up this statement:

Cash on hand..........................	$69
Due from C D..........................	17
	$86
Less due to A B........................	12
Net worth of "Me"....................	$74

Thus by two different processes we obtain the same result: one by an historical account, tracing the growth of wealth by excess of earnings over expense, the accumulation of net surplus; the other, not by a current account but an instantaneous one, which at a given moment inventories the concrete results of the same struggle.

47. The summary of balances which was given above is usually presented in account form. On the left are the "assets," consisting of property and claims upon property. On the right are, first, all claims against the assets, designated as the "liabilities"; second, the remainder unclaimed, or the net assets free from liability, variously known as "proprietorship," "capital," "stock," or simply by the name of the proprietor.

This statement is known as a "balance sheet."

FIGURE 16

BALANCE SHEET

Assets		Liabilities	
Cash on hand..........	$69	Due to A B...........	$12
Due from C D..........	17	Proprietorship..........	74
	$86		$86

48. I can see no benefit in lumping the $12 and the $74 together and calling them all "liabilities." Those who use this expression often contradict themselves by saying that the proprietary account is the excess of assets over liabilities; but if the proprietary account is *one* of the liabilities there cannot be any excess.

49. This miniature specimen shows the relation and inter-dependence of accounts. They are not isolated but each is connected with others. When they form a system which provides for the recording of all occurrences within a given sphere of proprietorship they constitute a ledger, the embodiment of whose results is the balance sheet.

CHAPTER IV

THE TRANSACTION

EQUATION OF THE BALANCE SHEET—EQUATION OF THE TRANSACTION —SIX OCCURRENCES, OF WHICH EVERY TRANSACTION MUST CONTAIN AT LEAST TWO—EXAMPLES OF EACH—ANALYSIS OF TRANSACTIONS

50. We cannot at this point enter upon a full discussion of the balance sheet or of the accounts whose results it embodies, both very interesting subjects.

51. It is sufficient at present to say that a balance sheet is compiled from all the accounts of a ledger, or rather from all that are not self-closed, without residue. In theory it halts every account and makes it give up its balance for inspection; but immediately restores it. This restoration is naturally not to the side to which the balance had to be added but to the side originally preponderant. It may be to a new account space, everything being started afresh, or it may be in the same column below the lines (=), like the balance brought down in Figure 10. The accounts of A B and C D would then read thus:

FIGURE 17

DR.			A B			CR.
Feb. 2	Repaid him....	$75	Jan. 1	Loaned by him..	$100
Mar. 3	Repaid him....	13			
Apr. 16	*Balance........*	*12*			
		$100			$100
			Apr. 16	Balance........	$12

22

FIGURE 18

Dr.			C D			Cr.
Feb. 15	Loaned him....	$35	Apr. 10	Collected.......	$10
Mar. 5	Loaned him....	12	" 15	Collected.......	20
			" 16	*Balance*........	*17*
		$47			$47
Apr. 16	Balance........	$17			

In other words, the contents of the balance sheet are distributed into accounts of which they form the first items.

52. Recurring to the balance sheet, remember that it is an equation:

$$Assets = Liabilities + Proprietorship$$

and that ordinary balance sheets contain nothing else; everything goes under one of these heads.

53. The accounts, having been for a moment halted, their results inspected and restored, are now ready to resume their progress. What rule can be given for the recording of any future occurrence so as to place it unerringly on the proper side of the proper account? Naturally, any increment must be on the same side as the balance which it follows.

54. Any occurrence must be either an increase or a decrease of values, and there are three classes of values; hence there are six possible occurrences:

1. Increase of Assets
2. Decrease of Assets
3. Increase of Liability
4. Decrease of Liability
5. Increase of Proprietorship
6. Decrease of Proprietorship

55. Balances of assets belong on the debit (left) side; therefore increases are debits and decreases are credits.

56. Balances of liabilities are credits; therefore increases of liabilities are credits and decreases are debits.

57. Balances of proprietorship are credits; therefore increases of proprietorship are credits and decreases are debits.

58. We have therefore the six possible occurrences distributed as follows under debits and credits:

DEBITS	CREDITS
Entries on left side	Entries on right side
Increase of Assets	Decrease of Assets
Decrease of Liabilities	Increase of Liabilities
Decrease of Proprietorship	*Increase of Proprietorship*

59. We have now to show that in every transaction at least two of the occurrences must appear and that they must be on opposite sides of the above list. This may be done by going through the list and taking up each of the six.

1. Increase of Assets. Suppose cash to be received; unless some other asset is given in exchange, or some liability discharged, our total worth must have increased by that much. That is to say:

> *Debit* Increase of assets must either correspond:
>
> *Credit* $\left\{\begin{array}{l}\text{to decrease of assets,}\\ \text{to increase of liability, or}\\ \text{to increase of proprietorship.}\end{array}\right.$

We cannot get something for nothing; but the something given in the third case is not a material something but a *service* of some kind.

Increase of proprietorship by giving service is called "earnings" or "income."

2. Decrease of Assets. If we part with any of our assets, unless we either receive in return some other asset of equal value or cancel some liability thereby, we have to the same extent diminished our net wealth or proprietorship.

Credit Decrease of assets must either correspond:

Debit { to increase of assets, or
to decrease of liability, or
to decrease of proprietorship.

In the third event we have parted with something of value without any tangible return. This is called "outlay." There is a true return, but it is in service received; as services are not listed in our assets, any more than our bodies, our minds, and our skill, we must consider that the result is a simple subtraction from our net wealth.

3. *Increase of Liability.* If we run into debt, unless we get something for it, or, what is just as good, get out of another debt, we must so far as our tangible wealth is concerned have lost proprietorship. As increase of liability is of exactly the same effect as decrease of assets, we have a series similar to the second one.

Credit Increase of liability must be attended either:

Debit { by increase of assets, or
by decrease of liability, or
by decrease of proprietorship.

4. *Decrease of Liability.* The payment of debt may be effected by parting with some asset, or by incurring a new debt; or if by neither of these means, but by giving services, then the net wealth is augmented, just as in increase of assets.

Debit Decrease of liability involves either:

Credit { decrease of assets, or
increase of liability, or
increase of proprietorship.

5. *Increase of Proprietorship.* We may increase our wealth in the form of more assets or of less liability, both of which are debits.

Credit Increase of proprietorship corresponds to:

Debit { increase of assets, or
decrease of liability.

It may possibly correspond to a decrease of proprietorship, but this would be an ideal shifting or transfer entry. Thus, a sawmill being one of our assets, and it being desired to keep the earnings of sawing separate, we consider that the real estate, if let to a tenant, *would* bring a certain rent; we credit that rent as earnings of real estate but debit it as outlay on behalf of the sawing enterprise.

6. *Decrease of Proprietorship.* This is precisely the converse of the preceding and requires no further argument.

Debit Decrease of proprietorship is either:

Credit { decrease of assets, or
increase of liabilities.

It is thus established that any entry to the debit, or left side, calls for a like amount on the credit side, and vice versa.

60. A few examples may serve to indicate how transactions may be analyzed into the debits and credits of which they are composed:

1. I purchase merchandise for cash. There is an increase of assets in the department of merchandise. There must therefore be a corresponding decrease of assets, or an increase either of liability or of proprietorship, one of the three occurrences on the credit side. Evidently the first of the three is the true one and the entry is of the form:

Dr. Increase of Assets   Cr. Decrease of Assets

In the abbreviated wording ordinarily used this would read:

Assets   Dr. to Assets

But usually we specify more minutely what particular department of the assets, and consequently what account, is affected, i.e.:

Merchandise   Dr. to Cash

This is still further shortened to:

Mdse to Cash

or

Mdse/Cash

It is understood that without special designation the account on the left is the one debited and the one on the right is credited.

The view might very rationally be taken that as the proprietorship was increased by acquiring the merchandise and was decreased by parting with the money, therefore the two changes of proprietorship should have appeared in the account, giving the following entries:

Mdse/Proprietor
Proprietor/Cash

But it seems useless to record in the proprietor's account exchanges which do not either increase or decrease his net wealth. This is attempted in the system of logismography, but its utility is doubtful.

2. I purchase merchandise from John Jones on credit. As the acquisition of merchandise is a debit, we must select from the three kinds of credit and get the result:

Dr. Increase of Assets   Cr. Increase of Liability
Assets   Dr. to Liabilities
Mdse/John Jones

3. Received cash for salary. As cash is received, the debit must be an increase of assets. What is the credit? No asset

figuring in the balance sheet has been diminished; no indebtedness has been incurred. The result is a clear increase of proprietorship, earned by the rendering of service:

Dr. Increase of Assets   Cr. Increase of Proprietorship
Cash/Proprietor

But it is seldom that the account of the proprietor receives immediate credit for an earning. Greater benefit is derived by providing a number of temporary accounts which are credited with earnings on a plan of classification, during a certain period, so that a comprehensive view of the progress of the proprietor during that period is afforded. This transaction would doubtless be credited to Salary account:

Cash/Salary

4. We hold a mortgage which is not yet due for several years. The interest is due every half-year. One month has elapsed since the last maturity and collection of interest. Wishing to bring our accounts down to date, how shall we represent the fact that this one month's interest has been earned?

It might be claimed that there has been no income because the payment of interest has not yet become due. But by the same reasoning it might be proved that there is no mortgage debt, for that is not yet due. There is in fact an indebtedness from the mortgage debtor to us. It grows from day to day, though it may not be convenient to register it every day. It is an asset which has been acquired during the month, not by exchange for some other asset, but by rendering service. The service rendered is the use of our capital.

Though the indebtedness from the mortgagor to us is a personal debt, yet it does not rest solely upon his credit, but upon the security of the real estate. It is for several reasons advantageous to consider it as a special kind of asset and not class it with other debts receivable. The increase of proprietorship caused by services given of this particular kind may also have an account by itself. Thus we analyze the transaction as follows:

Debit. We increase our assets by acquiring a claim for this accrued interest in addition to the principal debt.

Credit. We do not diminish any asset nor incur any liability by doing so; therefore we have an increase of proprietorship through the giving of service:

Accrued Interest/Interest
or Interest Earnings

5. We receive in payment of a debt partly cash and partly a note, or written promise to pay. Suppose that the debt is $200, the cash $50, and the note $150. Two kinds of assets are acquired, and one kind is parted with. We may consider this as two transactions or as one:

Cash/John Jones..................	$50	$ 50
Bills Receivable/John Jones.................	150	150

or

Cash/..........................	50	
Bills Receivable/John Jones.................	150	200

or in the old phraseology:

Sundries Dr. to John Jones.................	200
Cash.....................................	50
Bills Receivable..........................	150

61. It is not difficult to analyze a transaction into its debits and credits if we recall the six possible phases, three of debit and three of credit.

CHAPTER V

THE BALANCE SHEET

Its Importance—Its Constituents—How Constructed—By Inventory—By Derivation—Adjustments—Minuteness and Comprehensiveness to be Reconciled—Group Accounts—A Specimen Balance Sheet—Extended Meaning of "Debtor" and "Creditor"—The Reverse Method of Presentation—Equation of the Balance Sheet—Its Limitations—Order of Arrangement—Partnership Balance Sheet—Corporate Balance Sheet—One-sided Form—Business Without Balance Sheet—Municipal Accounts

62. The balance sheet may be considered as the groundwork of all accountancy, the origin and the terminus of every account.

63. The balance sheet of proprietorship is a summing-up at some particular time of all the elements which constitute the wealth of some person or collection of persons. It must comprise:

1. The values of assets, consisting of property and claims, to which the person, or collection of persons, has title.
2. The values of the claims existing against the assets and which must be satisfied from them.
3. The value of the residue after subtracting (2) from (1) and the respective proprietary interests in that value.

(1) = the sum of (2) and (3), and it is customary to place (2) and (3) together on the same side of an account.

(2) and (3) instead of being of the same nature (as is suggested when (3) is reckoned among the "liabilities") are sharply antagonistic.

64. The total value of the assets (not the assets themselves) is divided into two portions:

The portion subject }
The portion *not* subject } to outside claims.

30

65. There are two ways of constructing the balance sheet:

1. By actual investigation of quantities and prices of assets, and of extent of liabilities; also of distribution of proprietorship. In inaugurating a system of accountancy for a concern which has had no suitable accounts this is the only way. It may be called the "inventory" method.

2. By tracing the changes of values from the preceding balance sheet through the accounts, and collecting the resulting balances. This may be called the method by "derivation."

The former method is entirely independent of the books of account, the latter is entirely dependent on them and on their supporting vouchers.

66. If the books could be perfectly kept, the results would be the same by either method, just as the location of a ship by dead reckoning should theoretically coincide with that obtained by observation of the sun. We know that practically they always vary, and practically no system of accounts is so minutely accurate or so presciently devised as to take account of all changes and contingencies.

67. In practice, the two methods of constructing the balance sheet must co-operate. The results derived from the current accounts must be subjected to the scrutiny of valuation and even if they are purely matter of account like indebtedness, they should be verified by evidence from the negotiant whose interest in the balance is adverse to ours, or from an impartial source.

68. In the current work of accounts many records are provisional and intended to be subject to adjustment later. As the work must go on without interruption, there is necessarily a degree of roughness which can be corrected in the following balance sheet and which until that time does no harm. Hence to make the balance sheet as nearly perfect as possible adjustment must be made.

69. The question now arises: Should these adjustments be effected by supplementary entries in the current accounts or should they be ignored in the regular books and only appear through their influence on the balance sheet?

70. I should decidedly prefer the former course as making the results of valuation and derivation coincide; at least for a balance sheet which is intended for the information of the proprietors. Where a balance sheet or report is required by some outside authority, it may be that the point of view required is so alien to that assumed in the accounts themselves that no adjustment is practicable; they are constructed on a different basis. Nevertheless, even in this case the specially made adjustments should be left on record so that every figure in the report may be traced, if need be, to some figures of the books.

71. While every account is tributary to the balance sheet, yet it is very seldom that each account is represented by a separate balance. The balance sheet is almost always condensed by grouping into a single item many balances of similar nature. Thus, if the proprietorship has among its assets claims against various debtors, they are not set down at length in the balance sheet:

AB................ $........
CD................   ....
EF................   ....
etc................ $........

but are condensed into a single line:

Sundry Debtors............ $........

72. This gives a more comprehensive view of the business at the moment, but a less minute one. The minuteness is attained by means of a separate list, or schedule, giving in as full detail as may be required the facts of each individual account, and showing that the aggregate balances equal the single item recorded in the balance sheet.

73. All through accountancy runs the demand for minuteness and the contrary demand for comprehensiveness. They are generally satisfied by a double presentation. In organizing this, it is most satisfactory to make the condensed balance sheet *very* condensed so as to give a bird's-eye view of the general character of the business and to go to the other extreme in the expanded lists, giving all details that can be required.

74. In order to furnish both grades of information, to supply the broad results of the condensed balance sheet and the exact details of the individual accounts, two different grades of ledger may be kept. In the higher or more condensed ledger, accounts are kept with whole groups of assets or liabilities considered as a whole. For example, if there are among the assets numerous investments on mortgage, there is a single account entitled "Mortgages" in the general ledger while each separate mortgage has a separate account in a special ledger called the "mortgage" ledger. The balances of the mortgage ledger always equal, when aggregated at any given time, the balance of the Mortgage account in the general ledger, provided this latter is fully posted. This proviso is necessary because, while the mortgage ledger should always be kept posted to date, the general ledger may be further condensed by having its debits and credits entered monthly in a lump.

75. These group accounts are artificial. The members have no concert of action and no joint interests. The account exists solely for the convenience of the proprietor.

76. We now give a condensed balance sheet of the affairs of one James Jones in the form ordinarily used in this country, Scotland, and continental Europe:

FIGURE 19

BALANCE SHEET OF JAMES JONES

Dr.			Cr.
Cash................	$3,506.74	Mortgage.............	$4,000.00
Merchandise...........	22,166.73		
Personal Debtors.......	15,972.15		
Real Estate..........	10,000.00	*James Jones*..........	*47,645.62*
	$51,645.62		$51,645.62

3

We have placed the abbreviations "Dr." and "Cr." over the two sides which is the customary, though not invariable, rule, and we must interpret those expressions.

77. Looking at the left-hand side, we see that it consists of three kinds of property, and a collection of debtors. The property does not *owe* Mr. Jones anything; it *belongs to* him. Yet the balances of property are on what we agreed to call the debit side; there is a close analogy between property actually in possession and that which someone is bound to deliver to you; sometimes, as in case of a bank balance, it may be considered either property or debt receivable, at will. Let us, therefore, extend the meaning of the word "debtor" so that it means, when speaking of property, "belonging to," "the property of." To be consistent, the meaning of "creditor" must be extended correspondingly so that it means "owner of," as well as "owing to."

78. With these extended meanings, we may rewrite the balance sheet with interpretations.

FIGURE 20

BALANCE SHEET OF JAMES JONES
[Relations of Persons and Property to Him]

Dr.		Cr.	
[Debtors owing him or property belonging to him]		[Creditors claiming from him or his actual ownership]	
Cash [belonging to him]..	$3,506.74	Mortgage [owed by him]	$4,000.00
Merchandise..........	22,166.73		
Personal Debtors [owing him]...............	15,972.15		
Real Estate [belonging to him].............	10,000.00	*James Jones [what he is worth free and clear]...*	*47,645.62*
	$51,645.62		$51,645.62

79. Another form of presenting the affairs of Jones is just the reverse of the above. Instead of being the account of everybody else in relation to Jones, it represents Jones as he stands in relation to others; exhibiting him as creditor for what he owns as well as for what is due him, and on the other side what he owes as well as the resultant or that amount which he does *not* owe.   (Figure 21.)

80. This manner of presentation is mostly used in England— liabilities and ownership on the left, assets on the right.

81. When we say "in account with" between two names, we mean that the former is the debtor on the Dr. side and creditor on the Cr. side.   Thus, "A in account with B," means that the left-hand side of the account is *contra* A and the right side is *pro* A, while "B in account with A" reverses the sides.

FIGURE 21

JAMES JONES

[His Relations to Persons and Property]

Dr.		Cr.	
[Showing how *he* is indebted and what he is worth]		[Showing how *he* is creditor or owner]	
Mortgage [he owes].....	$4,000.00	Cash [he owns].........	$3,506.74
		Merchandise [he owns]..	22,166.73
		P e r s o n a l Debtors [he being the creditor]....	15,972.15
		Real Estate [he owns]...	10,000.00
[Balance or] *Net Capital*............	47,645.62		
	$51,645.62		$51,645.62

82. With these interpretations, we may describe these two modes as follows:

The American mode represents:

THE UNIVERSE IN ACCOUNT WITH JONES

The English mode represents:

JONES IN ACCOUNT WITH THE UNIVERSE

It seems to me that the American mode is preferable, for the following reason: "Jones in Account with the Universe" has already an account, like the one in Figure 14, which is a current account, not an instantaneous one; one which does not give a snapshot of his status but the history of how he arrives at that status. It seems to me that to have the instantaneous account and the historic account both from the same point of view is less logical than to assemble the accounts of the universe *including* that of Jones and show that the result is true.

83. But the mode, or order, is comparatively unimportant; the really vital thing is that we have an equation weighing assets on the one side against liabilities *and* proprietorship on the other. Jones expresses the same facts whether he chooses to say:

What Belongs to me + What is Owing to me =

What is Claimed from me + What is Unclaimed

or

What I Owe + What I am Worth =

What I Have + What I Claim

whether he writes in the third person or in the first.

84. The balance sheet has limitations. The personality of the proprietor, his skill, his experience, though important elements of his capital, can never be brought into his balance sheets. They cannot be bought nor sold and they only make themselves manifest through the services which he does sell.

85. The assets of the balance sheet consist solely of material factors outside of the proprietor, or of rights over others; in other words, of material things *now* in possession and of material things which *shall be* in possession.

86. The "Me" account, which almost invariably occurs, receives various names, and these indicate a feeling of difference between this account and the others. There is in fact a profound difference as between soul and body; between any man's Ego and Aliquis.

The most usual title for a sole proprietor's account is probably:

JAMES JONES, CAPITAL ACCOUNT

Another form is simply:

CAPITAL [ACCOUNT]

The objection to this is that all, or nearly all, of the assets are *capital* in the economic sense; the man or the group of men use both *loan-capital* and their *own capital* for their profit.

If we are careful to discriminate between the bookkeeper's "Capital" account, and the economist's "capital," no harm is done. If "James Jones' Capital" account is spoken of, this confusion is avoided. So it is if we borrow from the economist the terms, "capital-balance" or "net capital."

87. "Stock" is an old-fashioned word for the same meaning, but is now seldom used except as to corporations.

88. "James Jones, Proprietor," or "James Jones, Proprietary," would seem appropriate forms of speech for this purpose, though not much used.

89. The arrangement of the items in the balance sheet is of some importance, especially if the list is voluminous. There should be some governing principle applied throughout if possible. In our example the order of *availability* has been followed, or, as it might be termed, the order of *liquidation*. Those assets are given first which are most readily convertible into cash. On the other side, those liabilities should first be stated which must first be met, and lastly the proprietary interests which are entitled to no fixed sum but to "what is left."

90. It is not certain in any particular case that this order of presentation would be the best to follow. In an industrial enterprise where it was thought that productivity or earning power was more important than readiness in debt-paying, it might be that the fixed plant was entitled to the first place among the assets and that the cash on hand would be placed at the end as the least productive of assets. But, at any rate, *some* principle of arrangement is better than haphazard.

91. Let us now assume that James Jones, whose balance sheet we have exhibited, associates with himself William Smith as a partner under the firm name of Jones & Smith; also that Smith contributes a net proprietary interest of $23,822.81, viz., the following assets:

Cash	$5,082.34
Merchandise	17,082.65
Personal Debtors	8,123.17
Bills Receivable	7,000.00
	$37,288.16

subject to the following liabilities:

Bills Payable	$8,000.00
Personal Creditors	5,465.35
	$13,465.35

92. The firm of Jones & Smith is a unit in mercantile affairs. The assets belong now to both jointly; the debts have been assumed by both and both are responsible for their payment.

A new business entity has been created distinct from Jones and from Smith; it is a collective unity, but a real one. Professor Irving Fisher in his "Nature of Capital and Income" says that it is a "fictitious person holding certain assets and owing them *all* out again to real persons." In this I think he has been misled by the lazy habit of bookkeepers in calling all the credit balances liabilities, although they know that some of those balances are not liabilities. Even admitting that there is a fictitious entity it *owes* nothing to the real owners. It merely is a composite ownership which again is *owned* in various shares by real owners, and has nothing to do with debt.

93. The copartnership of Jones & Smith has a status at this moment; it therefore has a balance sheet. In this, the proprietorship may be represented jointly or distributively, as may be preferred. The former would be preferable for an outward balance sheet, such as to a mercantile agency, or in applying for credit; the latter for information of the partners. (Figures 22 and 23.)

FIGURE 22

BALANCE SHEET OF JONES & SMITH

Cash................	$8,589.08	Bills Payable.........	$8,000.00
Merchandise..........	39,249.38	Personal Creditors.....	5,465.35
Bills Receivable........	7,000.00	Mortgage Payable......	4,000.00
Personal Debtors.......	24,095.32	*Jones & Smith (the firm's*	
Real Estate..........	10,000.00	*capital)*.............	*71,468.43*
	$88,933.78		$88,933.78

FIGURE 23

BALANCE SHEET OF JONES & SMITH

Cash................	$8,589.08	Bills Payable.........	$8,000.00
Merchandise..........	39,249.38	Personal Creditors.....	5,465.35
Bills Receivable........	7,000.00	Mortgage Payable.....	4,000.00
Personal Debtors.......	24,095.32	*James Jones*..........	*47,645.62*
Real Estate..........	10,000.00	*William Smith*........	*23,822.81*
	$88,933.78		$88,933.78

94. Let it be supposed that Messrs. Jones & Smith, instead of a partnership, had preferred to form a company, named the "Jones Mercantile Company." They consider that, as the actual value of their joint proprietorship is over $71,000, it would be quite proper to capitalize it at $60,000, in 600 shares of $100 each. Nevertheless, there is a total proprietorship of $71,468.43, as before, all of which must be represented in some form.

In order to represent both the amount of the capitalization and the true proprietary value, we divide the total proprietorship into two parts:

Capital: par, or face value of shares........ $60,000.00
Surplus: excess of real value over par....... 11,468.43
Their sum is the real proprietorship........ $71,468.43

The resulting balance sheet would be:

FIGURE 24

BALANCE SHEET OF THE JONES MERCANTILE COMPANY

Cash.................	$8,589.08	*Capital Stock*..........	*$60,000.00*
Merchandise...........	39,249.38	*Surplus*...............	*11,468.43*
Bills Receivable.......	7,000.00	Bills Payable..........	8,000.00
Personal Debtors.......	24,095.32	Personal Creditors......	5,465.35
Real Estate...........	10,000.00	Mortgage Payable......	4,000.00
	$88,933.78		$88,933.78

95. The anomaly, not infrequently occurring, of ranking the capital and surplus *before* the liabilities may originate in the fact that a new corporation begins with capital stock and assets before contracting liabilities. It would seem more rational to place the proprietary accounts after the liabilities.

96. Another kind of business entity is now introduced, a collective body but still personal and real. The fictitious feature is the nominal or par value of shares. Jones holds 400 shares out of 600; this does not express the value of the shares but merely the proportion which they bear to the entire proprietorship. The true value of Jones' shares is not $\frac{400}{600}$ of $60,000, but $\frac{400}{600}$ of the entire $71,468.43, or whatever the true value may turn out to be. The *book value* of each share would be $119.11405 and this would vary with the ups and downs of business.

97. A distinguished publicist, Edward M. Shepard, has recently argued that it would be better if no nominal value at all were attached to shares of stock, if each merely represented the $\frac{1}{600}$ or the $\frac{1}{1000}$ part of the entire proprietorship. There could then be no such thing as watering, or its opposite.

98. As it is, however, the true net value of the concern is artificially split into two parts in order to exhibit the nominal capitalization. This is convenient for several reasons. The law generally strives to make the nominal capitalization conform to the cash originally invested. The nominal value of the share is a convenient basis for stating dividends by percentage. In some kinds of corporations, also, as insurance companies, the value is required to be kept up to at least the par of capitalization. In others, as national banks, shareholders are guarantors of solvency up to the par value of their shares, after those shares have fallen to zero.

99. The selling value of the shares should be, apparently, the book value of the assets minus the liabilities. Yet, no matter how accurately the assets may be valued and the liabilities ascertained, it is very seldom that the selling price corresponds to the book value. The reason may be that while the assets are sufficient for liquidation at the book value, they are not handled with the success which will earn the average rate of dividend. This may be from lack of skill, from unfortunate location, or some other disadvantage. But the purchaser is trying to buy future income, and will not invest unless he sees a prospect of getting it. On the other hand, the management of the business may be so successful that its earning power is greater than the average per dollar and if this is appreciated it will command a premium greater than the surplus.

100. The two-sided debit and credit form is not invariably the best for the balance sheet. To place the assets, liabilities, and net proprietorship one below the other is a very clear way of presentation, and admits of various orders of sequence, and of any process of summation.

101. We have said that there are certain assets, such as skill and experience which, in practice, never appear in the balance sheet. As a consequence there may be persons or business entities which have no balance sheet. An individual receiving a salary for his skill in some particular function and expending it exactly as fast as it is received, needs no balance sheet. His skill

is a non-ledger asset, and he accumulates nothing concrete.   If he does "get ahead" or "get behind" to a slight extent he will have assets and liabilities which will give rise to a balance sheet; but this will be insignificant in comparison with the non-ledger assets of personality + skill.   Nevertheless he requires outlay and income accounts, for he receives and gives services emanating from these non-balance sheet assets.

FIGURE 25

Net Worth of Investment...............................	$71,468.43
Liabilities...	17,465.35
Total Assets...	$88,933.78

DETAILED BALANCE SHEET

Capital Stock, 600 shares of $100................	$60,000.00	
Surplus....................................	11,468.43	
Net Value of Investment............................		$71,468.43
Assets:		
Cash......................................	$8,589.08	
Merchandise.................................	39,249.38	
Bills Receivable.............................	7,000.00	
Personal Debtors.............................	24,095.32	
Real Estate.................................	10,000.00	
Total Assets...		$88,933.78
Liabilities:		
Bills Payable..............................	$8,000.00	
Personal Creditors.........................	5,465.35	
Mortgage Payable..........................	4,000.00	
Total Liabilities......................................		$17,465.35

102. A municipal corporation is in a similar position.   Its principal asset is its power of confiscating the property of its members and others within its limits, through taxation, to an extent which cannot be valued, but which is measured by the needs, as legally ascertained, of its members.   In theory it is merely an agent for converting property into service.   It has assets and some of them can be valued; but the most important ones, like

highways, yield public and non-measurable service. It has liabilities also; but no balance can be struck between its assets and its liabilities which will define its status to any instructive purpose. Lists of its assets so far as ascertainable are valuable; lists of its liabilities are even more so; but its proprietorship cannot be reduced to dollars and cents and hence its balance sheet is non-existent. The highest function of municipal bookkeeping is the co-ordination of revenue and expenditure, of sacrifice and service. (See MacInnes, on Municipal Balance Sheets.)

103. Having thus established the foundation of the balance sheet, we will proceed to the analysis of its components, assets, liabilities, and proprietorship, all three of which are usually but not invariably present. Of these the most concrete and tangible are the properties and rights constituting the assets; next are the deductions or reservations therefrom known as liabilities, and finally, existing only as a relation, is the still more abstract conception of proprietorship.

104. The credit side gives the distribution, not of the actual assets but of their *value*, while the debit side divides them according to their nature. No one asset need correspond to any particular liability. The assets and liabilities taken together, the former being tangible and the latter definite, constitute the *specific* values which are the subject of the *specific accounts*.

CHAPTER VI

PHASES OF THE ASSETS

THINGS AND RIGHTS—INTERCONVERTIBLE—UNCOMPLETED CONTRACTS
—EMBODIMENT OF SERVICES GIVEN—STORAGE OF SERVICES TO BE
RECEIVED—CAPITAL—INVESTMENT

105. The specific values on the asset side of the balance sheet
are of two classes:

1. Things.
2. Rights.

Or we may say:

1. Things belonging to us.
2. Debts owing to us.

Or again:

1. Possessions.
2. Expectations.

We shall see upon examination that these classes imperceptibly
blend into each other and that every asset may be looked upon
either as a "thing" or as a "right."

Possession of a thing is merely the *right* to use it and
control it.

Therefore all our "things" may be looked upon as merely
rights of dominion. We look upon our cash as a thing and as
one of our most concrete assets. Yet the greater part of it is
usually in bank deposits, which are merely the *right* to receive
money on demand or to transfer such right to anyone who will
accept it instead of money. But excluding bank deposits as not
being money, we may hold bank notes or greenbacks. These
are nothing but printed agreements conferring the *right* to re-

ceive money, which is seldom called for. Finally, the coin, even if of the standard metal, is value in possession. Yet, unless we are jewelers, we do not *use* it. We prize it simply because we have the *right* under the law to satisfy contracts by parting with it.

106. Thus things convert themselves into rights, and the reverse is true: rights are convertible into things. Rights are but the future tense of things. Not only this but they are almost always secured by things. The personal indebtedness which we list in our assets is generally based upon the goods which were ours but which we have sold. We feel that they are still in existence as morally ours until paid for. We have trusted the purchaser for the reason that he owns these and other goods which will more than satisfy our claim. Thus all rights rest ultimately upon things, either present or expected.

107. But rights are sometimes materialized into a kind of artificial things, especially when they are evidenced by some material thing, such as a written document. A mere debt is seldom thought of as a thing in possession, while a note, which is a written acknowledgment of the same debt, is looked upon as something valuable in itself, because it can be touched and handled. Especially is this true of bonds, mortgages, etc., formal documents, usually transferable, which create the illusion that they are actual property, not merely the symbol of a debt.

On the other hand, things are sometimes personified into personal debtors, and the whole system of assets and liabilities is converted into a set of debts either receivable or payable. It is feigned that the Cash account is the account of the cashier; he is indebted for all the receipts and credited for all the payments. Similarly the warehouseman is regarded as owing for all the merchandise, the land agent for all the real estate; regardless of the fact that there is no actual indebtedness, since these custodians take no title to the things. Neither the shepherd nor his dog is in debt for the sheep.

108. These extremists, who have tried on the one hand to convert all assets into things, and on the other hand to reduce all things to personal debts, have had long discussions, especially in Italy, dividing themselves into the two camps of the *materialists* and the *personalists*. Apparently it has not occurred to these controversialists that in truth some of the assets are of the one and some of the other nature, and that many may be looked at in either phase; furthermore that so long as the nature of the asset and its form of account are understood, it is needless to twist it into the shape of some other asset. To seek the truth and follow the facts is safer than to compress everything into the mold of a "theory."

109. Rights always arise from uncompleted contracts. No man owes you unless there has been a contract, tacit or expressed, oral or written, for him to give you something and for you to give him something. If one of you has fulfilled his part of the contract, that one has acquired a right and the other has incurred an obligation. The contract may be a mere understanding without words, or it may be duly signed, sealed, and witnessed.

110. In another aspect all assets are the embodiment of services previously given; and in still another they are a storage of services to be received. Someone must have given labor in order to produce any wealth; but if it will not in the future command the services of labor, or save the expenditure of labor, or of its embodied results, it is worthless and not wealth at all.

111. Yet the values resulting from these two aspects are only approximately equal. On the one hand, the services which were given may have been sold for more or less than a just price as settled by competition; consequently the assets received for the services may be less or more than the future services receivable. The whole economic struggle (reducing everything to terms of service) is to sell one's own services high and buy the services of others cheap. On the other hand, a disservice (to use Professor Fisher's word) may have occurred through various causes, so that the services once anticipated appear impossible of entire realization. It must be observed that the aspect of assets as the present worth of future services is entirely based upon opinion, while the aspect which regards them as the resultant of services given is based upon facts.

112. Capital is defined by economists as that portion of wealth which is set aside for the production of additional wealth. In the balance sheet of a business concern, frequently, all the assets are capital, being employed as tools for its operations. There may be other assets, called "investments," where the actual handling of the tools is turned over to someone else and the value receivable for the services is returned in cash or other assets. This is exemplified in the ownership, by corporations, of the shares or bonds of other corporations. The physical assets underlying these securities are used as tools by the corporation issuing them, rather than by the one owning them. Yet in a remoter sense such vicarious assets may be considered as capital; for example, their possession may be a safeguard against some contingency or a reserve of strength. Hence it is easy to accept the view of Professor Irving Fisher, that all assets are capital.*

113. To summarize this chapter, the assets comprising the debit side of a balance sheet may be considered in one or more of the following ways:

1. As things possessed, directly or indirectly, or physical assets.
2. As rights over things and persons, for use, for services, or for exchange.
3. As incomplete contracts, whereof our part has been performed in whole or in part; or contractual assets.
4. As the result of services previously given, or *cost*.
5. As the present worth of expected services to be received.

---

* In the "summation of capital," Professor Fisher eliminates, by cancellation, the securities of one concern held by another, as they cannot furnish capital to both; which approximates to the distinction in the text.

6. As capital for the conduct of business operations.

7. As investment in the hands of another who uses it as capital.

114. The special case in which certain assets are devoted to the payment of certain liabilities will be treated under liabilities in the next chapter.

CHAPTER VII

PHASES OF LIABILITIES

115. As we pass from the asset side of the balance sheet we
seem to leave the actual and concern ourselves with the ideal;
the objective gives place to the subjective.   While the asset side
contains concrete actualities, the other side deals with the distribution of these actualities among those who have the title *to* them
and those who hold claims *against* them, the liabilities.

116. In algebraic language we may say that liabilities are
negative assets and that proprietorship is measured by the algebraic sum of all the assets positive and negative.

Another way of expressing this phase is that the liabilities are
postponed decreases of the assets; a future diminution having
the same effect on the net proprietorship as a present diminution.

117. The liabilities may to some extent be looked upon in
aspects corresponding to those stated for the assets, although
they never represent concrete property.

As rights, they are the rights of others against us and our
property, just as the assets are our right against others.

Considered as uncompleted contracts, they are those in which
our part of the contract is the part unfulfilled.

As capital, they represent that portion of the total capital
which has been furnished by others, or loan-capital.

118. Ordinarily there is no designation of certain assets as
destined to meet certain liabilities, but any or all of the assets
may, upon default, be expropriated to a sufficient extent to **pay**

any liability.   The word "assets," meaning "enough" or "sufficient," suggests this view of their nature from the point of view
of the creditor.   There are cases, however, where definite assets
are paired off against definite liabilities, in such a way that these
particular assets cannot be parted with unless the liability (which
is said to be "secured") has first been paid.   A familiar example
is the mortgage on real estate.   The title is in the owner; the real
estate stands in his balance sheet as an asset; he has full dominion
over it; he can collect the rent from it and can even sell the property subject to the paramount rights, or *lien*, of the mortgage.
The status of the property would be as follows, for example:

Value of Real Estate......	$10,000	Mortgage................	$4,000
		Equity.................	6,000
	$10,000		$10,000

The true proprietorship in the real estate is the "equity" in
the above balance sheet, and this is all that the owner can really
sell.   Hence, instead of calling the entire $10,000 an asset and
the $6,000 a liability he sometimes prefers to eliminate the
liability and treat the equity as a net asset.

Equity in Real Estate:	
Value $10,000, Mortgage	
$4,000.................	$6,000

The word "equity" in the balance sheet is taken in the
proprietary sense; here, in the sense of an asset.

119. Similarly, other assets are pledged to the satisfaction of
liabilities and usually some steps are taken to prevent the owner
from alienating the asset to the detriment of the pledgee.   The
United States government takes from national banks their bonds
as security for the redemption of circulating notes guaranteed
by the government.

Assets	Liabilities
. . . .	. . . .
. . . .	. . . .: .
U. S. Bonds to secure Circulation. . . . . $	Circulation (Notes outstanding) . . . .
. . . .	. . . . $

The ordinary loan on collateral is another example of an asset paired against a liability.

120. While there is this correlation between assets and liabilities taken in pairs, there is seldom exact identity of value. The asset is always taken, or intended to be taken, larger than the liability, for prudential reasons; so that there is a residue above the liability such as the equity in the mortgaged property or the margin in the loan on collateral.

121. Many seeming liabilities are more properly defined as deductions from certain correlated assets; of this we shall speak more fully under the head of offsets.

122. While assets may shrink in value, that shrinkage affects the proprietorship, never the liabilities, which must be regarded as rigid and inelastic.

CHAPTER VIII

PROPRIETORSHIP

123. The proprietorship may, like the liabilities, be viewed in the same phases as the assets, all except that of "things." Where there are any liabilities, no list of things can be drawn up which represents the proprietorship because the liabilities may be canceled by disposing of whatever assets are chosen for disposal by the proprietor. But if there are no liabilities whatever, the sum of the assets is the total proprietorship. Let us agree in the balance sheet at Figure 19, that the mortgage shall be stricken out and the value of the equity alone be carried as an asset. There being then no liabilities, the proprietorship is simply the sum of the assets and the balance sheet needs but one side:

Cash	$3,506.74
Merchandise	22,166.73
Personal Debtors	15,972.15
Equity in Real Estate	6,000.00
Capital	$47,645.62

The last line is proprietorship; it is capital in both senses, the bookkeeping sense and the economic sense.

124. As "rights," however, the proprietorship may be viewed. The assets being regarded as composed of rights against others and the liabilities as others' rights against us, the excess of rights in our favor is the proprietorship.

125. Thus the right-hand side of the balance sheet is entirely composed of claims against or rights over the left-hand side. "Is it not then true," it will be asked, "that the right-hand side is entirely composed of liabilities?" The answer to this is that the rights of others, or the liabilities, differ materially from the rights of the proprietor, in the following respects:

1. The rights of the proprietor involve dominion over the assets and power to use them as he pleases even to alienating them, while the creditor cannot interfere with him or them except in extraordinary circumstances.

2. The right of the creditor is limited to a definite sum which does not shrink when the assets shrink, while that of the proprietor is of an elastic value.

3. Losses, expenses, and shrinkage fall upon the proprietor alone, and profits, revenue, and increase of value benefit him alone, not his creditors.

For these reasons the proprietary interest cannot be treated like the liabilities and the two branches of the right-hand side of the balance sheet require distinctive treatment.

126. Considered as the effect of service, the proprietorship is the expression of how much more service has been given than received. Considered as the embodiment of future service it represents the net value of the service which the proprietor has a right to expect without giving any further service of his own.

127. Considering all the assets as capital, the proprietorship is that portion (in value) of the capital, which the proprietor furnishes as distinguished from the portion which he induces others to place in his hands for utilization, or the liabilities.

128. Before collecting the various phases of the assets, liabilities, and proprietorship into a systematic whole, it may be well to mention two somewhat fictitious methods of presentation, each introducing an intermediary element which disappears by cancellation.

129. In the cash theory, every transaction is supposed to pass through the phase of cash. There is no direct exchange of any asset for another asset, but it is assumed that cash is received for the former and at once paid for the latter. Thus a sale of merchandise on credit is represented as a sale for cash accompanied by a loan of the cash to the purchaser.

Purchaser/Mdse

becomes

Cash/Mdse
Purchaser/Cash

130. A very large number of the transactions are genuinely cash, and it is evident that the others may be separated into two each, one involving a receipt of cash and the other an expenditure. Without at present dwelling on this, we may conclude that any asset, except cash itself, may be considered to have cost money, and that any liability or proprietorship may be considered as having procured money or as being sources of money. The debit side of the balance sheet is transformed into a statement of cash paid, and the credit side into a statement of cash received —a reversed cash statement.*

131. Taking the figures of Figure 23 we thus transform them into the following:

FIGURE 26

BALANCE SHEET OF JONES & SMITH

Proceeds of Cash Paid		*Sources of Cash Received*	
For Merchandise.......	$39,249.38	From James Jones.....	$47,645.62
" Bills Receivable....	7,000.00	" William Smith....	23,822.81
" Personal Debtors...	24,095.32	" Bills Payable.....	8,000.00
" Real Estate........	10,000.00	" Personal Creditors	5,465.35
" Balance unpaid....	8,589.08	" Mortgage Payable	4,000.00
	$88,933.78		$88,933.78

* For a special study of the Cash account, see Appendix, Monograph A.

Jones and Smith are supposed to have paid in to the firm's treasury the sums which each was worth, and the firm to have also borrowed the sums of $8,000, $5,465.35, and $4,000, as stated. The firm then bought with the cash thus acquired the assets of each partner, which restored to each enough to replace in his private treasury the cash he had contributed and also to pay the individual debts, which are now replaced by the firm's indebtedness. There also remains unexpended a cash balance of $8,589.08.

132. The application of the cash theory to the corporate balance sheet (Figure 24) may serve to explain several things:

FIGURE 27

JONES MERCANTILE COMPANY

Capital and Liabilities		Assets	
[Cash received from]		[Cash paid for]	
Capital Stock..........	$60,000.00	Merchandise..........	$39,249.38
Surplus..............	11,468.43	Bills Receivable........	7,000.00
Bills Payable..........	8,000.00	Personal Debtors.......	24,095.32
Personal Creditors.....	5,465.35	Real Estate..........	10,000.00
Mortgage Payable.....	4,000.00	Cash Balance..........	8,589.08
	$88,933.78		$88,933.78

The facts for which this offers a plausible explanation are the following:

1. That the English accountants usually place the assets (cash paid) on the right-hand side and vice versa, this being the natural form of a cash statement.

2. That, as remarked in Chapter IV, the proprietary accounts usually come before the liabilities, companies being formed by first paying in cash for shares, in form at least. Often this is effected by the giving of checks which offset each other or are indorsed back, but the form is generally observed.

Assets	Liabilities	Proprietorship
Property	Deductions from property	Net property
Rights against others	Obligations to others	Surplus of rights
Assets	Negative Assets	Net Assets
Services heretofore given	Services heretofore received	Surplus of services rendered
Services expected to be received	Services which must be given	Surplus of services receivable
Capital	Loan-capital	Own capital
That for which cash has been given } Cash	Sources from which cash has been received	
Debtors to The Business	Creditors of The Business	

3. That the cash stands last in the list of assets, it being regarded as a balance unexpended.

133. The other theory adopts as its intermediary a supposed entity "The Business." All assets are regarded as "owing" to The Business and The Business is regarded as owing all the "liabilities," in which are included the proprietary claims. This is a favorite theory in this country, and it has this merit that it recognizes that the proprietor or proprietors may have many other investments and do not in the accounts presented reveal anything more than their worth as to The Business. But I cannot see that it justifies the inclusion of proprietorship among the liabilities. Surely The Business does not stand in the same relation to its proprietors or its capitalists as to its "other" liabilities. It would seem more appropriate to say that it is "owned by" than "owes" the proprietors.

134. On the preceding page are shown the phases which the three parts of the balance sheet assume from the different standpoints.

CHAPTER IX

OFFSETS AND ADJUNCTS

SUPPLEMENTARY ACCOUNTS; THEIR PURPOSE—OFFSETS AGAINST ASSETS —ADJUNCTS TO ASSETS—ADJUNCT TO PROPRIETORSHIP—OFFSET TO PROPRIETORSHIP SELDOM REVEALED

135. It is sometimes desirable for some special reason to separate the account of an asset, of a liability, or of a proprietor into two accounts, usually in order to present two different valuations. We shall call the supplementary account an *offset* or an *adjunct* to the principal account, according as it is intended to be subtracted from or added to the principal account.

136. As an instance of an asset take a set of machinery which cost a year ago $130,000. It is estimated that this machinery will be worthless in a few years, that is, that in those years its value will pass from $130,000 to 0. It is also estimated that the first year of use will depreciate the machinery to the extent of 20 per cent, or $26,000. If it is desired to keep a record of the original cost, $130,000, and at the same time of the present worth, $104,000, it may be done by using two accounts on opposite sides of the ledger:

Machinery at cost, $130,000   Depreciation, $26,000

This depreciation is not a liability, although it is frequently listed among the liabilities, but an offset to the asset. In a correctly constructed balance sheet it would not appear except indirectly in this form:

Machinery			....
Cost........	$130,000		
Depreciation	26,000	$104,000	....

137. In Chapter VII there was a discussion of the relation between a piece of real estate and the mortgage upon it. Two forms of stating the accounts were presented:

(a) Real Estate..........	$10,000	Mortgage................	$4,000
(b) Equity in Real Estate: Value $10,000, Mortgage $4,000........	6,000	....	

In case (b) the $4,000 is eliminated as being merely an offset, while in (a) it is treated as a liability.

138. It may be noted here that it is not quite a matter of indifference which of these forms is used, but that the facts may be different. If the owner bought this property *subject* to the mortgage, so that he cannot be held for a deficiency judgment, then it is quite appropriate to treat the mortgage as an offset and the equity only as the true asset. If, however, he gave his note or bond for the $4,000 it would be more correct to keep the mortgage standing by itself as an actual liability.

139. While offset accounts are kept in their current state for convenience, it is proper that at the date of the balance sheet they should be eliminated by subtraction from the opposite side. Adjuncts, being already on their proper side, do not give the same trouble, whether they are left in the main column or added in the margin.

140. As an adjunct to an asset, take the case of a bond purchased at a premium, the par value being $75,000 and the premium paid being $6,131.79. It is desired to exhibit both the par value and the total cost, $81,131.79. For this purpose two accounts may be carried and in the balance sheet they may both be exhibited or their sum:

(a) Bonds at par.........................	$75,000.00	
	Premium...........................	6,131.79
(b) Bonds at cost.......................	81,131.79	

141. As an offset to a liability we may take the case of a note (bill payable) for $6,666.67 which has just been discounted at 3 months at 5 per cent per annum. It is desired to keep an open account of the face of the note (the sum which must be paid three months hence), and also of the actual proceeds. This is done by means of a Discount account, an offset to bills payable. The actual proceeds are $6,583.34, and this is all that at the beginning of the three months is owing; as the three months pass the liability rises till it reaches $6,666.67 at maturity. The accounts at first represent the condition thus:

Discount, $83.33   Bills Payable, $6,666.67

Many bookkeepers consider the discount as lost or "disserved" at once, not gradually. Scientifically, at least in theory, it should be assumed that the liability is at first $6,583.34 and gradually rises, through the accretion of adverse interest, to $6,666.67, which latter sum is composed of $6,583.34 borrowed + $83.33, interest at 5.0625 per cent.

142. The balance sheet in Figure 24 gives an example of an adjunct to a proprietary account. The true capital balance is $71,468.43, but it is divided into the two parts, $60,000, the par value of the shares, and $11,468.43, the surplus.

143. On the other hand let us suppose that the nominal capital had been fixed at $75,000, which would really have been nearer the truth than $60,000. The $3,531.57 by which the capitalization exceeds the true value would then be an offset against the $75,000 and two accounts would have to be carried:

Deficiency, $3,531.57   Capital Stock, $75,000.00

144. This is theoretically correct but in practice you will seldom see such a frank confession of impaired capital. Almost universally the assets are hoisted to meet the exigency, or the deficiency is represented as an asset. This receives some euphemistic title, such as "Good-Will," "Franchises," "Patents." This may not be with any fraudulent intent, but from a feeling that the latent personal assets, spoken of in Articles 84 and 101 as "non-ledger" assets, make the concern worth at least par as a revenue-producer. There is a natural reluctance to admit the fact of overcapitalization or "watering."

CHAPTER X

INSOLVENCY

145. The converse or negative of *proprietorship* is *insolvency*. When the assets exceed the liabilities, the difference is proprietorship, or net wealth; when the liabilities exceed the assets the difference is negative wealth or insolvency. The equation of the balance sheet will then appear as:

$$\text{Assets} + \text{Insolvency} = \text{Liabilities}$$

146. Even those who contend that proprietorship is among the liabilities would scarcely claim that insolvency is an asset. In actual practice, however, it is seldom admitted that there is a state of insolvency. Precisely as in the case of impaired capital, treated in the last chapter (Article 144), some alleged asset is inserted to swell the total assets to a state of at least solvency, from the same motives as those cited in that article.

147. It is possible that, notwithstanding the balance sheet exhibits a state of insolvency, there may be earnings which at least equal the outlay, thus leaving the insolvency or deficit unincreased.

It is even possible that there may be a surplus of earnings which tends to cut down the deficit. This will indicate the existence of latent (non-ledger) assets (Article 84) overcoming the deficit, and in that case the creditors will be encouraged to permit the concern to go on, that course being advantageous to them.

148. There are four possible cases of status as to solvency and the power to improve the situation (barring exact equilibrium):

1. Solvent and gaining.
2. Solvent but losing.
3. Insolvent but gaining.
4. Insolvent and losing.

149. If the creditors are aware of the facts, their attitudes under these four suppositions will be as follows:

1. They have neither the right nor the disposition to interfere with the management.
2. They have no right to interfere but will have the disposition to enforce their claims in advance of impending insolvency, if possible.
3. They have the right to interfere but will be disposed to refrain from doing so.
4. They have both the right and the disposition to interfere with the management by the proprietor and will endeavor to displace him.

150. When this displacement is put into effect, it is done through the agency of an intermediary, usually a representative of the courts, whose duty it is to administer the assets and as far as possible to discharge the liabilities. His balance sheet will not be a proprietary but a fiduciary one, as will be explained later.

CHAPTER XI

THE PERIOD

151. The balance sheet might be taken at any moment or at any irregular interval of time; but in order that the events during one interval may be profitably compared with those of another, the intervals should be equal. It is therefore desirable not only to make the periods between balances equal, but to make them correspond to the astronomical divisions of time, upon which human activities so much depend. Therefore the day and the year are the minor and the major units of time most frequently employed as accounting periods.

152. The day is the smallest accounting unit of time recognized. Commercial transactions on the same day are regarded as simultaneous, and obligations are generally performable, not at a certain hour, but merely on a certain day, at an optional hour. When the hour is specified, as in fire insurance and rent, it does not apply to the financial transaction but to the physical fact, conflagration, or possession which determines it.

The legal day is from midnight to midnight. The business day is from the beginning of business hours to the end.

153. From any part of the business hours of one day to any part of the business hours of the next day is one day, not two. Therefore the number of days is really measured by the number of intervening *nights*, or by subtracting the numerical designation of the initial date from that of the final date.

154. As the date from which reckoning is made is excluded, the proper way of designating the year is "from the 31st of

December, 1906, to the 31st of December, 1907," rather than "from the 1st of January, 1907, to the 1st of January, 1908." This latter expression would really mean 364 days in 1907 and 1 day in 1908. To be quite definite it is better to say "from the 1st of January to the 31st of December, *inclusive*."

155. From the rule of excluding the day *from which*, it follows that all transactions of a certain date are to be considered as occurring at the close of business on that day. Balance sheets are sometimes dated as of the day at the beginning of which the status exists and sometimes are given the date at the end of which it exists, the same balance sheet being dated indifferently "December 31, 1907," or "January 1, 1908." I regard the former as the more correct for the reason given above and also because the balance sheet is more significant as the result of the work of 1907 than as the inception of 1908.

156. In some of the old writers a balance at the *beginning* of the first day of a month was designated by a zero date; thus the closing balance of 1906 would appear as "December 31, 1906," while the same balance at the opening of 1907 would be dated "January 0, 1907," a quaint but logical distinction.

157. A daily balance sheet is not unknown; but usually it is informally made up without disturbing the routine of the accounts to which it remains external. It must largely depend upon estimate rather than realization; or else the accidental fluctuations will be so great as to destroy its utility.

158. The year is the most natural and usual period of accountancy. The calendar year, January to December inclusive, is an easy period for reference, though for many businesses December 31 is not a natural epoch of conclusion. Quite frequently a date is selected at which there is least activity in the business itself and most leisure for the labors attendant upon the balancing process.

159. An intermediate unit, such as the quarter or the month, is often chosen for the purpose of summarizing the work and comparing it with the same unit in previous years.

160. The major unit, from balance sheet to balance sheet, is usually the year, sometimes the half-year, seldom the quarter-year. The intermediate unit is almost always the month, occasionally the week, seldom the quarter; a special period of 28 days is sometimes used so as to embrace even weeks. When the half-year or the quarter is the balancing period, two or four of them are easily combined, giving the yearly history.

161. When I have occasion to speak of these periods, it will be of the *year* as the major unit of time or balancing period, and of the *month* as the intermediate or summarizing period, although in fact the former may be a half-year or the latter a week.

162. The use of a monthly grouping of transactions has this special advantage for keeping a general ledger and subordinate ledgers (Article 74): the general ledger may contain only monthly entries in aggregate, while the subordinate ledgers contain separate transactions day by day. The general ledger will be more condensed and more generalized, with saving of labor.

CHAPTER XII

ECONOMIC ACCOUNTS

163. The whole purpose of the business struggle is increase
of wealth, that is increase of proprietorship. The counterpart of
increased proprietorship is either increased assets or their equivalent, diminished liabilities, as shown in Article 59 (5). We may
in discussion ignore the case of diminished liability and consider
all increase of proprietorship as manifested in increase of assets,
which increase might be immediately utilized in discharge of
liability.

164. While increase of wealth is taking place, it is almost
always attended by a partial decrease, a parting with assets in
the expectation of ultimately recovering assets of greater value.
These decreases are offsets to the increase, but for analytical
purposes are usually kept, in the first instance, separate.

165. The all-important purpose of the proprietary accounts is
to measure the success or failure in increasing wealth, and to
analyze that success or failure so as to ascertain its causes, as a
guide for future conduct.

166. Increases and decreases of wealth, so far as they arise
from business conduct, are, therefore, not recorded immediately
on the accounts of proprietorship but in subordinate accounts.
Each of these subordinate accounts represents a class of events
in the business conduct dependent on a common cause, as Mer-

chandise Profit, Interest, Discount, Rent, Insurance, Salaries, Expense, Freight, Taxes. Whenever any increase or decrease of wealth is realized or recognized it is recorded, according to its nature, in one of these subordinate accounts, which we shall call, as a whole, the "economic accounts."

167. Mere accessions of capital not earned but contributed do not belong in the economic accounts. An example of this is given in Article 91, where Smith brings in additional capital but no economic change takes place.

168. The economic accounts should run for a definite time. It must be kept in mind that they are tributary to the proprietary accounts and that they withhold certain records for the purpose of an analytical summary. No comparison of one of these summaries with another can be useful unless they cover an equal time. The rate of progress must be ascertained by obtaining a common denominator in time. It is therefore the best accounting practice to keep economic accounts open for the year (or balancing period) and then, with the greatest nicety, carry the net result into the main proprietary account, which in the meantime has stood still awaiting the returns of its subordinates.

169. Thus, by an ingenious and somewhat artificial system of economic accounts, the highest possibilities of accountancy are attained. Without the analysis here described, it would hardly be worth while to maintain any proprietary accounts, at least for a sole proprietor. Omitting the proprietary and economic accounts would leave what is generally known as "single entry."

170. The accounts of assets and liabilities, as we have already said, are the specific accounts. They might also be called the "exterior" accounts, as they alone affect persons outside of the business, while the proprietary and economic accounts are the "interior" ones, kept for the instruction of those inside. The economic accounts may therefore be kept with a freer hand than the specific; their subdivision, the plan of their arrangement, the decision as to the treatment of doubtful (or "border-line") cases are entirely at the option of the proprietors.

171. Where it is a question of more or less minute subdivision, the more minute is usually the safer, because it is easier to remedy overminuteness by combination than to reanalyze what is found not minute enough. It is easier to mix wine and water than to separate them.

172. The ordinary forms of ledger account may be abandoned altogether for the economic accounts and some form of tabulation substituted, which will often exhibit the results far more effectively. The metaphoric conceptions of debtor and creditor may be totally discarded here where they have less pertinency than in any other class of accounts. These accounts have nothing whatever to do with indebtedness, but represent on their respective sides:

LOSS	PROFIT
EXPENSE	GAIN
CHARGES	REVENUE
OUTLAY	INCOME
	EARNINGS

All these synonyms are used in various connections with slightly varying shades of meaning, but their general purport is:

DECREASE OF WEALTH	INCREASE OF WEALTH
for services received	for services given

173. Unless care is taken to include in the economic entries of a period all that properly belongs in it and to exclude all that pertains to any other period before or after, we may greatly distort the presentation of facts so as to render it valueless; the period which has been adverse may appear prosperous at the expense of one which is actually more successful. The question must always be asked: Is there any residual asset or liability at the beginning or at the end of the period which has not been taken into account?

174. Many consider that there is no income until received in cash and that there is no outlay until paid in cash. Suppose one of the large expenses of a business is the cost of coal. Coal is ordered and put into the bins in January, say 200 tons, and paid for in February, at $5 per ton. It is used up as follows: in January, 30 tons; in February, 26 tons; in March, 31 tons.

175. Those who treat everything as being outlay at the time of cash payment would make no entry in January; in February the entry:

Coal [expense]/Cash.............................. $1,000

The economic summaries for these three months would then indicate the cost of coal as follows:

For January...................................... 0
February...................................... $1,000
March...................................... 0

January and March would be relieved from all expense for coal although the coal was used right along, and those months would appear as very profitable but February as most disastrous.

176. Another bookkeeper might think proper to credit the dealer as soon as the coal is received and charge him when paid for:

Jan. Coal [expense]/Coal merchant.................. $1,000
Feb. Coal merchant/Cash......................... 1,000

This is more correct than the cash statement, for it recognizes the purchase at its proper date. But there is again a false distribution of the cost. The entire cost of the coal is merely shifted to January, and that month stands all the burden, while February and March go free.

177. The error is in considering the coal as instantly consumed when paid for or when received. The true cost in such a case is the value consumed, the residual coal being an asset.

178. When the coal was purchased, it was all an asset. Coal, as an expense, was the quantity burned:

Jan. Coal [asset]/Coal dealer...................... $1,000
" Coal [expense]/Coal [asset]................... 150
Feb. Coal dealer/Cash........................... 1,000
" Coal [expense]/Coal [asset]................... 130
Mar. Coal [expense]/Coal [asset].................. 155

FIGURE 28

COAL [ASSET]

Jan.	Purchased 200 tons...	$1,000	Jan. Consumed	30 tons...	$150
			Feb. "	26 tons...	130
			Mar. "	31 tons...	155
			" Balance	113 tons...	565
		$1,000			$1,000

COAL [EXPENSE]

Jan.	Consumed...........	$150
Feb.	"	130
Mar.	"	155

179. If no record of the coal consumed has been kept, we should have to resort to taking an inventory of the amount on hand and thence inferring the consumption.

FIGURE 29

COAL

Jan.	Purchased 200 tons...	$1,000	Mar. 31	Balance as per Inventory 113 tons.........	$565
			Jan.-Mar.	Consumption....	435
		$1,000			$1,000
Apr. 1	Balance..........	$565			

180. This is an account of coal as an asset and also of the consumption of coal as an economic fact, the latter being inferred from the former. The first presentation in Article 178 furnished a check upon consumption of coal; the quantities issued from the storehouse being known, the balance on hand *should* be 113 tons and any deviation from that quantity indicates error or defalcation. In this latter presentation there is no check on the inventory.

181. If the coal had been purchased in small quantities as needed, say, about 10 tons a week, the purchases would have been so nearly in accord with the consumption that no great error would be made in considering the coal as an expense as soon as bought.

FIGURE 30

COAL [EXPENSE]

Jan.	1	10 tons............	50	
"	8	10 "	50	
"	15	10 "	50	
"	22	10 "	50	
"	29	10 "	50	
Feb.	5	6 "	30	
"	12	6 "	30	
"	19	6 "	30	
"	26	6 "	30	
Mar.	5	8 "	40	
"	12	10 "	50	
"	19	10 "	50	
"	26	10 "	50	
			560	

In this account, unadjusted, there is an error of $125, or rather a neglected asset of that value. In modern accountancy, no such errors even if minute are allowed to stand over into the next period, but an adjustment is made rectifying both the consumption and the residue.

182. The only absolutely correct rule is to base the outlay account, not on the receipt of the supplies nor on the payment for them, but on their consumption, and it should be apportioned as to time accordingly, either by a regular account of consumption, checked by an inventory, or by inference from the inventory.

183. It may be asked whether the same rule applies to supplies having almost no *salable* value, such as business stationery designed especially for a certain particular concern. Perhaps there has been considerable expenditure for engraving, printing, ruling, binding, etc., and yet this would be a dead loss for purposes of sale, the value being actually below that of the blank paper. The residual asset, it might therefore be argued, is practically nothing. But this is not quite correct; for selling purposes on liquidation, its value would be nothing, but to go on with, it has its full proportionate value. If a year's supply was bought and enough remains in good condition to last a half-year longer, then half the total cost has been consumed and half remains as an asset. Its value as an asset consists in relieving us from the necessity of expending anything further for the same purpose for months to come. For this purpose it is as good as the cash.

184. This question of two valuations, one for liquidation, the other for a going business, frequently arises. I am of the opinion that *in* a going business the latter is the balance to be carried, because only in that way can the true economic outlay or income be ascertained. This is not the same case as that of the depreciation of plant, which is a normal charge and should be provided for out of income; it is the case of current supplies being made "second-hand" by the process which adapts them to their purpose.

185. Rent paid in advance is a valid asset, whether it would have any selling value on winding-up or not. It is the right to occupy the premises for a definite time, without further payment. It is the remainder of a contract of which the lessee has performed all and the lessor only a part.

186. It frequently happens that the actual cash receipt or payment resulting from any economic source exactly coincides as to time with the consumption or accretion to which it corresponds. This coincidence must not make us lose sight of the fact that it is really the consumption or accretion of a right which we need to record in economic statements, not the settlement of the claim in cash.

187. This is particularly noticeable in those economic departments where the value is measured in time units (like interest and rent) rather than in volume units (like coal or gas).

188. Interest is usually payable in cash, semiannually. It is earned, however, continuously, the day being the smallest unit recognized. We will take the case of a mortgage loan for $18,000 at 5 per cent, due 3 years from May 1, interest payable semiannually on the first of May and of November. The balancing period is also semiannual, January 1 to June 30, inclusive, and July 1 to December 31, inclusive. This is the only asset on January 1, the loan being made as of that date. On May 1, 4 months' interest having accrued, $300 are collected on or soon after that day, and this is all during the half-year. The bookkeeper who deals only with cash would make the economic entry:

Cash/Interest...................................... $300

A balance sheet of June 30 would then show this result:

Mortgage...............	$18,000	Proprietor..............	$18,300
Cash....................	300		
	$18,300		$18,300

189. This result is incorrect; it shows that the proprietor on a 5 per cent investment has received or benefited only at the rate of 3 1/3 per cent.

190. In fact, the mortgage loan is not now an asset of $18,000 but of $18,150. The mortgage paper not only secures the payment of $18,000 a few years from now but it secures just as firmly the right to interest at the *rate* of 5 per cent per annum. The $150 is just as valid an asset as the $18,000. The objection will be made that the $150 is not due and may never be collected; the reply is that the $18,000 is not due either and we might as well strike it out of our assets.

191. Instead of the interest entry given above the following would have been correct:

Mortgage/Interest [earnings]....................... $450
Cash/Mortgage.................................... 300

FIGURE 31

BALANCE SHEET

Mortgage..............	$18,150	Proprietor..............	$18,450
Cash.................	300		
	$18,450		$18,450

192. This represents the facts correctly, but in practice it is preferable to keep the Mortgage account at par or principal, and make an adjunct account of the interest which has been earned. "Interest Receivable" will be a distinctive title for this, which is really a portion of the mortgage debt, and the entries will be:

Interest Receivable/Interest [earnings]................ $450
Cash/Interest Receivable........................... 300

FIGURE 32

BALANCE SHEET

Mortgage [principal]......	$18,000	Proprietor..............	$18,450
Interest Receivable.......	150		
Cash.................	300		
	$18,450		$18,450

Interest Receivable may be subdivided into Interest Accrued and Interest Due, as will be explained under assets, but that distinction is not now in question.

193. In the following half-year the earnings will be $450 and the cash receipts $450, but this is merely coincidence; the $450 cash is not collection of the $450 earned. It is the collection of $150 for May and June, and of a part, $300, of the July-December interest.

194. On the cash plan, the last half-year, in which the mortgage falls due, would show an apparent earning of $450 instead of $300; an error equal and opposite to that of the first half-year.

195. This question of Outlay and Income, as opposed to Receipts and Payments, is one which frequently arises in practice. It has often been discussed as to municipal accounting. Those who contend that there is no income until it is collected in cash seem to forget that this reasoning would prevent us from making any record of sales except cash sales; also that one of the objects of public accountancy is to test what is received by what *ought* to be received.

196. The cash receipt or payment is not the cause of the increase or decrease of proprietorship, but the effect, although in point of time it may precede. The cause of the economic event is service given or received and it may just as well be embodied in any other asset, usually in a right, as in cash. It is therefore short-sighted to look upon the cash transaction as originating the entry.

197. If a cash statement is the only record extant of the transactions of a period, it may be, and should be, converted into an Outlay and Income account by adjustment. This account, as derived from cash, is mixed, partly specific and partly economic. The adjustment consists in inserting such balances as are known to be specific, both at the beginning and at the end of the account.

198. For example, the Interest account based on the transactions in Article 188, would be a mixed account, partly representing claims against persons for interest and partly representing the economic result or increase of proprietorship through interest. Only by adjustment can we separate these.

FIGURE 33

INTEREST

	Jan.-June Collected......... $300
	July-Dec. Collected......... 450

As adjusted and ready for transfer to the Proprietorship account:

FIGURE 34

INTEREST

June 30	*Net Income*........	*$450*	Jan.-June Collected..........	$300	
			June 30 *Accrued*..........	*150*	
		$450		$450	
July 0	*Accrued*...........	*$150*	July-Dec. Collected..........	$450	
Dec. 31	*Net Income*........	450	*Dec.* 31 *Accrued*...........	*150*	
		$600		$600	
Jan. 0	*Accrued*...........	*$150*			

199. The net income here appears, as it should, equal in the two periods. All that is printed in italics is adjustment. Having inserted at the beginning and end the ascertained balances the resultant is the economic result to which the proprietor is entitled. By a coincidence, the result in cash and the economic result in the second period appear the same; but, as already explained, they are equivalent, not co-extensive.

200. An economic account is, normally, one-sided. That is, it should represent *either* outlay or income, not both. Mixed accounts, such as an Interest account which represents on the one side Interest Cost and on the other side Interest Revenue, are not generally to be commended. The two sets of events had better be kept distinct unless they are in fact correlated. The "off" side of an economic account is better reserved for offsets or corrections, of the normal side. A mixed account of this kind may sometimes require in its adjustment a double balance, an asset being brought down to the debit and a liability to the credit.*

The economic accounts should comprise the regular outlays and incomes forming part of the economic scheme, and judgment must be used in laying out these accounts. For example, loss by bad debts is in some businesses so improbable that such a catastrophe is made the subject of a special entry. On the other hand, in other kinds of business a current economic account is required for "Bad Debts" as a normal incident of the business, under that or some other name. There are then three ways of treating worthless accounts: (1) by transferring them bodily to this account; (2) by merely marking them with some symbol, crediting an offset account to the same amount; (3) by crediting a reserve based on the percentage of experience as a general offset.

201. It would be desirable if the titles of accounts could indicate by their form whether they were primarily intended to be specific or economic. As any economic account may give a specific residue and almost any specific account may yield an economic resultant, it is not usual to make such distinction in titles. But it is sometimes very useful to do so, as, for example, in the interest accounts. Interest Receivable, Interest Due, Interest Accrued, Interest Payable are assets or liabilities, from which the economic accounts Interest Cost and Interest Revenue should be clearly differentiated.

---

* For a special study of the Merchandise account, which as formerly kept was a mixed account, see Appendix, Monograph B.

CHAPTER XIII

THE ECONOMIC SUMMARY

202. At the close of the period, the economic accounts, reduced to their simplest terms, must be transferred into the proprietary accounts, as if they were receptacles for measuring the effects of various causes and were poured at the appointed time into the great reservoir. But as there are among them both positives and negatives it is found convenient to have an intermediate account, a summary of all their results. From this account of the second degree a resultant is obtained for distribution to the proprietary interests; and sometimes even this is not done directly but through an account of the third degree raised solely for the purpose of distribution. The freedom (already alluded to) of the interior accounts as to form, permits any device to be employed which will tend to a clearer view of the economic history of the period.

203. The account of the second degree, which I have called the "economic summary," is known in practice by various names: Profit and Loss, Loss and Gain, Trading, Outlay and Income, Revenue.

"Profit and Loss" is the most usual of these names. Two objections are made to it. The first is as to the order of the two nouns. Writing as we do from left to right, "profit" is brought on the left, whereas the right side is the one on which all profit is entered. It is claimed that instead of:

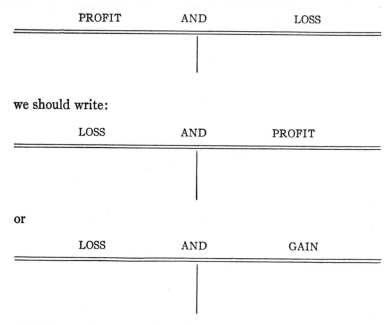

PROFIT   AND   LOSS

we should write:

LOSS   AND   PROFIT

or

LOSS   AND   GAIN

This I regard as a somewhat fanciful objection, the order of the words being suggested by our preference and expectation rather than by any intention of heading each side with a distinctive title.

204. The second objection is that the debits of such an account are not "losses" but are a necessary investment which is expected to be more than returned; they are values *laid out* with the expectation that they will later *come in*. From this point of view "Outlay and Income" would seem to be an appropriate title, agreeing with the location of the two sides of the account, and also indicating that outlay is always incurred before income is acquired.

205. We may consider the title "Profit and Loss account," however, as referring, not to the items composing it, but to the final outcome, which is either Profit *or* Loss. In this sense the time-honored title is entirely justified.

206. To present the affairs of a business concern at the close of a year in intelligible shape it is necessary to have these documents:

> A balance sheet at the end of the period, showing the then condition.
>
> A Profit and Loss account for the period, showing how the condition was attained.

There may also be presented:

> A balance sheet at the beginning of the period, which may be incorporated with the final balance sheet in side columns.
>
> Various schedules giving details of the contents of the foregoing documents.

207. For the sake of illustration we will take the business of the Jones Mercantile Company, whose balance sheet, say, on December 31, 1906, appears in Article 94. We desire to bring the history down to December 31, 1907, and to present a balance sheet and Profit and Loss account under that date.

The following are the economic accounts which it has been thought advisable to keep:

Sales. On the credit side of this account are entered the amounts of merchandise sold, at selling price. Ordinarily these would be entered in the Sales account in monthly totals only, the separate bills being recorded in sales books. On the debit side of the account is entered the cost of the sold goods, either in monthly or in yearly aggregate. The difference is the merchandise profit; it is debited to the Sales account as a result and credited to the Profit and Loss account. This result is $15,520.66. The company has given to its customers the services of bringing its stock of goods near their homes, of arranging them for selection, of hiring salesmen to exhibit them, of making public their good qualities and of transporting them to the homes of purchasers.

6

The payment for these services consists in the merchandise profit, $15,520.66.

Some of the services included in this profit must be paid for, reducing to that extent the profit of the company.

Salaries.   Direct payment for services of those employed in the business.   A debit entry to Profit and Loss of $4,000.

Delivery.   Payment to express companies and to messengers for delivering goods.   A debit of $987.56.

Freight.   This has been already comprised in the cost of the goods, the principle being that we reckon as cost all expenditures up to the moment the goods are on our shelves; thereafter as expense of selling.

Insurance.   The company paid premiums for insurance against fire, both on its goods and on its store, amounting to $169.50.

Interest Cost.   Interest has been or must be paid on the mortgage and on the bills discounted, amounting to $387.50.

Taxes.   The annual taxes assessed against the real estate, $151.42.

Repairs.   A similar charge against the real estate, $232.19.

Fuel.   On this account there may be a residue as illustrated in Article 178.   The amount actually consumed is $365.

Light.   This, being metered, leaves no residue and the entire amount, $279.50, is debited to Profit and Loss.

Supplies.   On this account again there is no residue, as the company takes all its supplies from its own stock, charging them at cost and only as fast as required.   Debit $463.84.

208. In addition to the profit on merchandise, there are some other sources of income which must appear to the credit of the Profit and Loss.

Interest Revenue.   At the middle of the year $5,000 were invested at 6 per cent, producing $150 interest.   It may be asked why this and the Interest Cost account should not be combined in a single Interest account, to be debited with $387.50 and credited with $150. This might be done and often is done, but in reality there is no connection between the two kinds of interest, and their difference, $237.50, has no distinct meaning.

Rent Revenue. The company lets a part of its building for $240 per annum.

209. Transferring the result of each of these accounts to a Profit and Loss account, we have as net earnings or increase of proprietorship, $8,374.15, the distribution of which is shown in the second part.

FIGURE 35

PROFIT AND LOSS

Outlay		Income	
Salaries..............	$4,000.00	Profit on Sales........	$15,520.66
Delivery.............	987.56	Interest.............	150.00
Insurance............	169.50	Rent................	240.00
Interest..............	387.50		
Taxes................	151.42		
Repairs..............	232.19		
Fuel.................	365.00		
Light................	279.50		
Supplies.............	463.84		
	$7,036.51		
Net Profit............	*8,874.15*		
	$15,910.66		$15,910.66
Dividend, $10 per share.	$6,000.00	Net Profit, brought	
Carried to Surplus......	*2,874.15*	down..............	$8,874.15
	$8,874.15		$8,874.15

SURPLUS

	1907	
	Jan. 0 Balance......	$11,468.43
	Dec. 31 Profit........	2,874.15
		$14,342.58

This subdivision of the economic summary into several stages is a modern and very useful invention of the British accountants.

210. The resulting balance sheet might be as follows:

FIGURE 36

BALANCE SHEET

At the beginning of business, January 1, 1908

Cash................	$7,643.59	Personal Creditors......	$5,745.83
Bonds...............	5,000.00	Bills Payable..........	7,000.00
Merchandise..........	44,262.83	Mortgage Payable......	4,000.00
Bills Receivable........	5,250.00	Dividends Payable.....	6,000.00
Personal Debtors.......	24,826.99		
Real Estate...........	10,000.00	Total Liabilities....	$22,745.83
Fuel.................	55.00	Capital Stock..........	60,000.00
Accrued Interest.......	50.00	Surplus..............	14,342.58
	$97,088.41		$97,088.41

In the above balance sheet the more natural order has been followed in placing the proprietary accounts last, which also admits of the insertion of the total of liabilities.

211. The Profit and Loss account submitted in Article 209 gives the correct result, but may be criticized in several respects. It does not show the profit made in the process of buying and selling as distinguished from the interest on securities which has nothing to do with merchandising. It also mingles the cost of maintaining the real estate with the shop expenses.

It will be a useful lesson in the construction of economic summaries if we reform this one so as to obviate the above objections.

212. We shall first open a Trading account, excluding from it all items which do not belong to the business of merchandising.

213. As to the real estate entries, upon consideration we see that the ownership of the property saves us the payment of rent. The insurance (so far as it relates to the building), the taxes, the repairs, the interest on mortgage, all these are a substitute for rent. Furthermore, there are $6,000 equity, on which, if we borrowed the money, we should have to pay 6 per cent interest. We open an account with Real Estate Expense and transfer to it all the above outlays by the following entries:

Real Estate Expense/Insurance (on real estate)......	$ 70.00
Real Estate Expense/Interest Cost (on mortgage)....	300.00
Real Estate Expense/Taxes......................	151.42
Real Estate Expense/Repairs.....................	232.19
Real Estate Expense/Interest Revenue..............	360.00

On the other hand, we have not used all the premises ourselves, but have let a part for $240, which reduces the rent cost to the company by that amount:

Rent Revenue/Real Estate Expense

When all these entries are posted, the Real Estate Expense account will appear as follows:

FIGURE 37

REAL ESTATE EXPENSE

Insurance..............	$70.00	Rent..................	$240.00
Interest on Mortgage....	300.00	*Carried to Profit and Loss*.	*873.61*
Taxes.................	151.42		
Repairs...............	232.19		
Interest on Equity [estimated].............	360.00		
	$1,113.61		$1,113.61

The expense as to real estate, which takes the place of rent, is thus reduced to the single item, $873.61. The last entry on the debit side is not actual, but hypothetical. It adds to the interest revenue artificially a sum which is also artificially added to the cost of rent. This shifting does not affect the final result, or net increase. Such transfers should be sparingly used, and with great care.

214. We now establish a Trading account, a general Profit and Loss account, and a Distribution account, and for illustration make them continuous, merely bringing down balances. We also insert, in the English style, the qualifications "Dr." and "Cr.," "By" and "To," which are occasionally met with in this country.

FIGURE 38

TRADING, PROFIT AND LOSS, AND
DISTRIBUTION ACCOUNT

DR.		1907		CR.
To Salaries............	$4,000.00	By Profit on Sales......		$15,520.66
" Delivery...........	987.56			
" Insurance [on stock].	99.50			
" Interest............	87.50			
" Fuel..............	365.00			
" Light..............	279.50			
" Supplies...........	463.84			
" Real Estate Expense in lieu of rent.....	873.61			
	$7,156.51			
" *Profit and Loss carried down*...........	*8,364.15*			
	$15,520.66			$15,520.66
To Distribution........	*$8,874.15*	By Trading, brought down.............		$8,364.15
		Interest.............		510.00
	$8,874.15			$8,874.15
To Dividend..........	$6,000.00	By Profit and Loss.....		$8,874.15
" Surplus...........	2,874.15			
	$8,874.15			$8,874.15

215. This highly technical form of presentation is less suitable for the information of the public and of those interested than the analytical statement shown in Figure 39.

216. Where it is possible, the bookkeeping should be so planned that the items for each economic account shall be grouped into monthly totals preparatory to posting to that account, instead of a long list of smaller items. This monthly grouping, which will be dwelt upon hereafter, is more important in these accounts than in the specific accounts. It is also desirable to eliminate corrections and offsets before the totals are carried to the final account. When this is done, the accounts of outlay and income can readily be thrown into a tabular or synoptical form.

FIGURE 39

SUMMARY OF THE ECONOMIC ACCOUNTS

From Page	1907		
	GROSS PROFIT on sales.................		$15,520.66
	OUTLAY:		
	Salaries............................	$4,000.00	
	Delivery...........................	987.56	
	Insurance on Stock...................	99.50	
	Fuel...............................	365.00	
	Light..............................	279.50	
	Supplies...........................	463.84	
	Interest............................	87.50	
	Real Estate Expense in lieu of Rent.....	873.61	
	Total............................	$7,156.51	$7,156.51
	NET TRADING PROFIT............................		$8,364.15
	Interest on Investments (including equity in real estate).		510.00
	Total Revenue.............................		$8,874.15
	DISTRIBUTION:		
	Dividend, $10 per share on 600 shares.............		6,000.00
	Increase of Surplus Account.....................		$2,874.15
	Balance of Surplus at beginning................		11,468.43
	" " at close...................		$14,342.58

217. This tabular form may assume either of the arrangements shown in Figures 40 and 41.

FIGURE 40
OUTLAY, 1907

	Jan.	Feb.	Mar.	Apr.	May	June	July	Aug.	Sept.	Oct.	Nov.	Dec.	Total
Salaries.........													
Delivery.........													
Insurance.......													
Fuel............													
Light...........													
Supplies........													
etc......													
Totals........													

FIGURE 41
OUTLAY, 1907

	Salaries	Delivery	Insurance	etc.	Totals
January......					
February.....					
March........					
April.........					
May..........					
June.........					
July..........					
August.......					
September....					
October......					
November....					
December....					
Totals......					

218. To carry out this plan in any particular case will perhaps require the introduction of special columns or lines for adjustment, but this general scheme of additions both down and across will give a more comprehensive view of the progress of the business than a number of disjected accounts in the traditional form.

CHAPTER XIV

THE TRIAL BALANCE

219. In any ledger, if every transaction up to a certain date has been fully and correctly posted, there must be an exact equality between the totals standing on the debit side and on the credit side. The initial balances, taken from the balance sheet, were in that state of equilibrium; and, as shown in Chapter IV, each transaction has added equal amounts to the two sides.

220. It follows also that if the balances, or resultants, of the several accounts were ascertained, they would also show the same equality. For in every account having amounts on both sides the process of balancing consists in canceling an equal amount on each side and this cannot affect the equilibrium of the entire system.

221. The equality of totals depends upon the mathematical principle that, if equals be added to equals, the wholes will be equal. The equality of balances depends upon the same principle and also upon this other: that, if equals be subtracted from equals, the remainders will be equal.

222. If it is found, however, that the sum of the totals, or of the balances, are *not* equal, there is surely an error in the contents of the ledger or in its summation or its balancing. But while inequality is a certain indication of error, equality is not a certain indication of correctness, for it is possible that equal amounts of error exist on the two sides.

223. A list of total debits and credits of each account or a list of debit and credit balances is called a "trial balance," and is intended primarily as a test of correctness. Many use it solely for that purpose, but it may be made to serve other uses and to take the place of an interim balance sheet.

224. The trial balance must be taken when the ledger is fully written up. As we shall explain hereafter, in the most perfected systems many of the transactions are only half-posted in the first instance, one item of the transaction being reserved to the end of the month and posted in aggregate. It follows that the most appropriate date for a trial balance is the end of the month.

It is quite usual to suspend all posting during the taking-off of the trial balance; but by affixing a special mark to the last entry, the posting routine may be kept up without danger of confusing the new matter with the old. The three-column ledger (Article 17, Figure 7) is very convenient for this purpose.

225. The usual form of a trial balance is as follows:

FIGURE 42

TRIAL BALANCE

Page	Name	Dr.	Cr.

The columns "Dr." and "Cr." may be filled either with totals or with balances.

226. By additional columns headed "Dr." and "Cr." in pairs, the trial balances for several months may be contained on the same page or pages, without the necessity of rewriting numbers and names of accounts.

227. In order to prevent the omission of accounts from the trial balance it is generally found best to enter them in the order in which they follow each other in the ledger. If this order is not systematic and logical very little use can be made of the trial balance except as a test of mechanical correctness in posting. In the modern unbound ledger, consisting of loose cards or leaves and admitting of shifting and rearrangement, the ledger can be kept in exact order; while in the bound book, unless a great deal of space is wasted in blank pages, the necessary filling-up and transferring to new pages is pretty sure to throw it into more or less disarrangement.

228. It may be thought preferable to arrange the accounts alphabetically, taking the names and pages from the index and then filling in the amounts from the account.

229. Where there is a system of subordinate ledgers (Articles 74–75) the trial balance, like the balance sheet, may profitably be condensed by entering only the aggregates. The subordinate ledger has its own subordinate trial balance which proves the correctness of its posting. Even if there be no such system of subordinate ledgers, an aggregate may be made up expressly for the trial balance of all the accounts of a homogeneous group, in a list or schedule only the total of which appears in a single line of the trial balance.

230. We will now give as an example of a condensed trial balance alphabetically arranged, the supposed trial balance of the Jones Mercantile Company using the same materials as in Article 210, and exhibiting both totals and balances.

231. A comparison of the balance column with the balance sheet in Article 210 will show that they are substantially the same. Had a small adjustment on account of fuel on hand been made before the trial balance was taken off, the only difference would be that the economic accounts stand with open balances instead of being closed into Surplus, of which they are really adjuncts and offsets.

232. When an accountant is called in, and wishes to obtain a rough statement of condition for prompt use, he may, if a recent trial balance is at hand, transform it into a statement of assets and liabilities by eliminating all the economic balances.

FIGURE 43

TRIAL BALANCE, JONES MERCANTILE COMPANY

December 31, 1907

Page	Name	Totals		Balances	
		Dr.	Cr.	Dr.	Cr.
	Accrued Interest....	$ 450.00	$ 400.00	$ 50.00	
	Bills Payable.......	3,000.00	10,000.00		$ 7,000.00
	Bills Receivable....	6,750.00	1,500.00	5,250.00	
	Bonds............	5,000.00		5,000.00	
	†Capital Stock......		60,000.00		60,000.00
	Cash.............	54,696.50	47,052.91	7,643.59	
	*Delivery..........	987.56		987.56	
	Dividends Payable..				
	*Fuel.............	420.00		420.00	
	*Insurance.........	169.50		169.50	
	*Interest Cost......	387.50		387.50	
	*Interest Revenue...		150.00		150.00
	*Light............	279.50		279.50	
	Merchandise.......	126,842.11	82,579.28	44,262.83	
	Mortgage Payable..		4,000.00		4,000.00
	Real Estate.......	10,000.00		10,000.00	
	*Rent.............		240.00		240.00
	*Repairs...........	232.19		232.19	
	*Salaries...........	4,000.00		4,000.00	
	*Sales.............	82,579.28	98,099.94		15,520.66
	*Supplies..........	463.84		463.84	
	†Surplus...........		11,468.43		11,468.43
	*Taxes............	151.42		151.42	
	Customers Ledger, Balances.........	24,826.99		24,826.99	
	Creditors Ledger, Balances.........		5,745.83		5,745.83
		$321,236.39	$321,236.39	$104,124.92	$104,124.92

He will run his pencil through all the economic accounts
(marked*) and the proprietary accounts (marked †) and
adding together the remaining amounts will form the following
statement:

FIGURE 44

Accrued Interest..............................	$50.00	
Bills Payable..		$7,000.00
Bills Receivable..............................	5,250.00	
Bonds......................................	5,000.00	
Cash.......................................	7,643.59	
Merchandise.................................	44,262.83	
Mortgage Payable.......................................		4,000.00
Real Estate...................................	10,000.00	
Customers Ledger.............................	24,826.99	
Creditors Ledger..		5,745.83
Total Assets................................	$97,033.41	
Total Liabilities.......................................		$16,745.83
Net Worth...		$80,287.58

If in the balance sheet, Article 210, we add together:

Capital.............................	$60,000.00
Surplus............................	14,342.58
and Dividend Payable................	6,000.00
we have the result....................	$80,342.58

The difference, $55, is the amount of fuel on hand for which no adjustment had been made.

233. The prevention, detection, and correction of the errors which are known to exist when the trial balance does not agree would naturally be the next subject to be treated of; but for practical reasons it would be better to defer its consideration until the make-up of the accounts is more fully discussed.

CHAPTER XV

THE JOURNAL

A Preliminary Book—Formerly Considered Indispensable and the Only Source of Posting—Analysis of Transactions—Form of Journal Entries—Balance Entries Through Journal—Certain Entries for Which the Journal Is Advantageous—Gradual Disappearance of the Journal—Auxiliary Books —Monthly Journalization of Auxiliary Books—Posting Delayed—Downfall of the Complete Journal

234. Thus far we have treated of accounts only, and in fact the account, in the broad sense in which I am using the word, is that for which all the processes of bookkeeping exist, all else being subsidiary to it. The tendency of modern accountancy is towards making all records perform the functions of accounts without any preliminary manipulation. But until some time in the nineteenth century, all entries in the ledger were *posted* from a preliminary book called the journal and therefore in an entry comprising a single debit and a single credit the same amount was written four times, twice in the journal and twice in the ledger. By skilful modifications of the method, the same material is now entered not oftener than twice.

235. But even the journal was not at first the original record. It had as its precursor the *day book*, which narrated the occurrence without any technical indication of the debits and credits to which it gave rise. Then the same material was put into technical form, or as it was said, "journalized," which was considered a momentous and difficult operation. Finally the entries in the journal were severally posted to the proper sides of the ledger accounts.

236. It was for a long time supposed that these three books, the day book, the journal, and the ledger, formed an indispens-

able triad; that without these three "principal books" there
could be no double-entry bookkeeping, and that all other records
were "auxiliaries" to these. The day book is now practically
abolished, and the journal nearly so. In modern times the
original entry is almost invariably in the form of some kind of
paper, document, or voucher, valuable as evidence. These
papers are, for all the normal, staple types of transactions, in
printed blanks and their form points out the place in the books of
account where they must be entered. This is practicable in
modern business, where labor is subdivided and an employee
performs only one, or a few kinds of functions; and it makes the
entries self-journalizing.

237. The journal was not, properly speaking, a book of account, but a book of detached entries to be formed afterwards
into accounts. In its original form, the amounts of the several
entries were not even added together, but subsequently this was
introduced.

238. In Chapter IV the analysis of transactions was treated
and illustrated. The journal entry expresses this analysis, stating the titles of the accounts to be debited, followed by the titles
of the accounts to be credited, the two being usually separated
by the words "Dr. to."

Thus a purchase of merchandise on credit was entered as
follows in the journal:

```
56   Merchandise Dr.
379      To A———— B————            $........
         for purchase of ............
         ...........of ...........at  $........
```

The marginal figures at the left indicate the *pages* of the Merchandise account and of A —— B ——'s account respectively,
to which the posting has been made.

239. Compound entries, that is, those containing more than
one debit or more than one credit—usually contained the word
"Sundries" which might easily have been dispensed with. Thus,

if Cash were to be debited and Bills Receivable and Interest were both to be credited, the phrase was:

<pre>
                 Cash Dr. to Sundries
for proceeds of note of A——— B——— $........
bearing interest, etc.
                    To Bills Receivable $........
                       " Interest   ....
                                             $........
</pre>

This is a very awkward form especially as it brings the name of the account to be debited far from the sum. The more modern form of journal, with two money columns for the debit and the credit amounts respectively, either with or without the words "to Sundries," is greatly preferable:

<pre>
Cash Dr. [to Sundries].......... $........
   To Bills Receivable........ $........
      " Interest................   ....
for proceeds, etc.
</pre>

240. The double money columns afford, through their totals, the power of ascertaining whether all the contents of the journal have been posted to the ledger, whereas in the detached form an entire entry might have been left unposted without affecting the trial balance. The total of the ledger should evidently equal the total of the journal if it has all been derived from that book, but to apply this test it is necessary to use the trial balance by totals (Article 219), not by balances.

241. In the rigorous application of the journal principle, every entry to the debit or credit side of the ledger must invariably come from the journal. This was carried so far that even the striking of the balance of an account and bringing it down was attended with the same formality. The entry would read:

<pre>
Smith & Jones, old account, Dr.
   To Smith & Jones, new account
</pre>

or

<pre>
Brown & Robinson, new account, Dr.
   To Brown & Robinson, old account.
</pre>

7

These would be posted as follows, the title of the account not being repeated:

Dr.	SMITH & JONES	Cr.
To new account.....		
....		....
	By old account.....	....

A debit balance is, of course, brought down in the reverse way.

242. A regular balance sheet was also the product of journalization under the name of the Balance account. All the transfers of assets to the debit side of the Balance account were effected through the journal, thus:

> Balance Dr.
>   To Cash
> Balance Dr.
>   To Merchandise, etc.

Each transfer of liability or proprietary account was likewise made to depend upon a journal entry:

> Bills Payable Dr.
>   To Balance
> Mortgage Payable Dr.
>   To Balance, etc.

243. It is evident that the result of posting these entries to a ledger account entitled "Balance" would be to construct a balance sheet on a page of the ledger. This would correspond in arrangement to the balance sheet used in most parts of the world outside of England, not the reverse form in Articles 79 and 80.

244. Usually this formality was considered sufficient and the reopening of the accounts was effected by simply *bringing down*

the balance to the opposite side as already exemplified in Article
51. But there were those who would have considered this abbre-
viation heterodox and insisted on restoring the balances by
journal entry. But here a distinction must be made; there must
be two balance accounts, the closing Balance and the opening
Balance, although the latter was usually merely a prolongation of
the former within the same lines. The opening Balance account
would be the "English" form of balance sheet, with assets on the
right.

245. The journal entry for the closing balance (Article 242)
was somewhat tedious as a complete entry was needed for every
separate account. The compound entries, "Balance Dr. to
Sundries" and "Sundries Dr. to Balance," were therefore employed to save labor. The result will be seen in the following
journalization of the closing entries which would bring out
the balance sheet of Article 76 in the form of a Balance
account:

Balance Dr. to Sundries.............	$51,645.62	
To Cash.......................		$3,506.74
" Merchandise.................		22,166.73
" Personal Debtors [group account]		15,972.15
" Real Estate.................		10,000.00
Sundries Dr. to Balance............		51,645.62
Mortgage........................	4,000.00	
James Jones.....................	47,645.62	

The entries for the opening balance would be debit where
these are credit and credit where these are debit.

246. Now, if we post these items exactly as given, the Balance
accounts will appear as follows:

Dr.		BALANCE		Cr.
To Sundries..........	$51,645.62	By Sundries..........	$51,645.62	
To Sundries..........	$51,645.62	By Sundries..........	$51,645.62	

This account is as nearly useless as it can be. It really gives no information as to the status, for which reference would have to be made to the journal, which in its legitimate use is not a book of reference but a source of material for the ledger.

247. No wonder then that some bookkeepers "cut out" the Balance accounts altogether and made a "Sundries to Sundries" entry as follows:

Closing Entry

Sundries Dr. to Sundries

Mortgage Payable.................	$4,000.00	
James Jones......................	47,645.62	
To Cash.......................		$3,506.74
" Merchandise.................		22,166.73
" Personal Debtors.............		15,972.15
" Real Estate.................		10,000.00

Opening Entry

Sundries Dr. to Sundries

Cash...........................	3,506.74	
Merchandise.....................	22,166.73	
Personal Debtors.................	15,972.15	
Real Estate.....................	10,000.00	
To Mortgage Payable............		4,000.00
" James Jones.................		47,645.62

248. Thus we see that the Balance account in the ledger was first made useless and finally eliminated altogether by reason of the inconvenience of the journal. But a modification in the form of the journal, which a few were bold enough to adopt, might have remedied this defect and enabled the Balance account to become a true balance sheet.

249. The most effective way to do this is to place the titles of the accounts in the center without dropping a line, and the amounts on the outside of the page. In this way the components of the balance sheet are posted in detail.

This form of journal is so much more compact and comprehensible than the old one, that in future illustrations it will be employed.

FIGURE 45

Amount Dr.	Dr.	Accounts December 31	Cr.	Amount Cr.
$3,506.74	Balance	Cash		$3,506.74
22,166.73	"	Merchandise		22,166.73
15,972.15	"	Personal Debtors		15,972.15
10,000.00	"	Real Estate		10,000.00
4,000.00	Mortgage Payable	Balance		4,000.00
47,645.62	James Jones	"		47,645.62

250. It is doubtful, however, if there is any utility in making closing entries on the journal, so far as balances are concerned. Having tested the accuracy of the posting and having adjusted any valuations requiring it, the balances may be simply brought down and transcribed into their proper places in the balance sheet.

251. There still remain certain interior transfers in which the journal is used to advantage:

1. Incidental transfers from one account to another, not comprised in the regular "run" of the business.
2. Opening entries expressing incorporation and capitalization.
3. Adjustment of values which have been roughly carried. This always changes specific value to economic, or vice versa.
4. Closing the economic accounts into a summary, profit and loss, or trading account.
5. Distributing the net income or loss to whom it may concern.

252. Cases 3, 4, and 5 may be illustrated by journalizing some interior transactions which may be supposed to result in a trading account.

1. A specific residue in an account which is normally economic.

$55.00........Fuel, new account........Fuel, old account........ $55.00
       for coal on hand as per inventory
50.00........Interest, new account......Interest, old account..... 50.00
       for interest earned but uncollected, etc.

The effect of the "old account" entries will be to increase the amount of the net earnings from these respective accounts.

2. Creation of a special economic account for ascertaining the cost in lieu of rent. The entries for this purpose have been indicated in Article 213.

3. Transfer of all economic accounts into a summary.

$15,520.66 Sales...................Trading............... $15,520.66
4,000.00 Trading.................Salaries............... 4,000.00
987.56 " ....Delivery.............. 987.56
99.50 " ....Insurance.............. 99.50
87.50 " ....Interest............... 87.50
365.00 " ....Fuel.................. 365.00
279.50 " ....Light................. 279.50
463.84 " ....Supplies.............. 463.84
873.61 " ....Real Estate Expense.... 873.61
   to close all outlay and income accounts relating to merchandise
$8,364.15 Trading.................Profit and Loss......... $8,364.15
     to close Trading account
$510.00 Interest.................Profit and Loss......... $510.00
     for income outside of mercantile business
$8,874.15 Profit and Loss.........Distribution.......... $8,874.15
6,000.00 Distribution............Dividends Payable...... 6,000.00
   for dividend declared December 27, at $10 per share
$2,874.15 Distribution............Surplus............... $2,874.15
    to close Distribution account.

253. By comparing these entries with the accounts in Article 209 it will be seen that the use of the journal might largely have been dispensed with, since the effect is merely analytical—a placing of the material in new combinations rather than the recording of any new acts or facts. The declaration of the dividend is the only administrative act which is recorded as taking place; all else is arithmetical process, which might have been carried on in the accounts themselves.

254. Beginning now with the original journal, which contained a record of every occurrence, one by one, we may trace its evolution and final disappearance.

255. It is very probable that, when the contents of the day book were translated day by day into the technical language of the journal, the process of condensation began by grouping together transactions of the same kind into a compound entry. Thus if there were on a certain day four persons who purchased goods on credit, the entry became:

$$
\left.
\begin{array}{l}
\$229.43 \ \text{A B} \\
100.00 \ \text{C D} \\
736.50 \ \text{E F} \\
29.84 \ \text{G H}
\end{array}
\right\} \quad \text{Merchandise.......} \quad \$1,095.77
$$

instead of:

$229.43 A B	Merchandise.......	$229.43
100.00 C D	"	100.00
736.50 E F	"	736.50
29.84 G H	"	29.84

Only one posting to the Merchandise account was necessary instead of four, and this one posting actually gave more valuable information than the four.

256. The next step in condensation was to break up the day book into several special books, such as the sales book, the invoice book (more properly purchase book), the cash book, each devoted to transactions of a certain type. The sales book contained only entries which would in the journal appear as debits to persons and credits to merchandise (or in more modern times to Sales account), and similarly with the invoice book and the cash book, leaving the day book merely for those few transactions which did not concern either cash or merchandise. If there still remained in the day book any other class of entries which recurred frequently enough to make it worth while, another book was opened for this class.

257. These books were called "auxiliary" books, the journal being still considered as the most important book, in fact, as *the*

book. Nevertheless vastly more information was obtainable
from the auxiliaries than from the journal.

258. As it was considered inadmissible that anything should
get into the ledger except through the journal, the contents of all
these auxiliary books had to be journalized, and this came to be
done monthly as the most convenient time.   The cash book gave
rise each month to two long entries:

Sundries Dr. to Cash

and

Cash Dr. to Sundries

the sales book became

Sundries Dr. to Merchandise
[or Sales]

the invoice book became an entry:

Merchandise Dr. to Sundries

and in this manner the day book contained only few exceptional
entries not provided for elsewhere.

259. This monthly journalization necessitated monthly posting but was attended by the inconvenience that the posting was
always in arrears, so far as related to the personal accounts.
These exterior accounts are the very ones which should be kept
closely up to date and to some extent they were always a month
behind.   Where the work was voluminous, the trial balance could
hardly be verified until a month after its date.

260. This inconvenience proved the downfall of the journal.
Probably the posting was short-circuited direct to the ledger
account, in advance of its being journalized, this posting being
considered as an anticipation of the regular process.

Since the auxiliary book contained a total, which could also
be posted directly, it became evident that the journal as such was
a superfluity.

CHAPTER XVI

POSTING MEDIUMS

261. The so-called "auxiliary" books instead of being subdivisions of the day book now became subdivisions of the journal.
It will be better to leave the name "journal" to the original
book, surviving in a limited sphere of utility, and call all the
books from which the ledger accounts are derived "posting
mediums."

262. The day book has now disappeared. The cash book is
used as a posting medium for all receipts and payments; the sales
book for all sales; the invoice book for all purchases. There
may also be bills receivable and payable journals; returned goods
books, both outward and inward; deposit books, draft books,
interest journals; in short, an infinite variety of special posting
mediums. In each, the separate items are kept posted from day
to day, while the monthly totals are posted to the opposite side in
a single sum. And this is the ideal result, for the exterior accounts should be kept perfectly posted up to the very moment,
while the interior accounts, kept for instruction, are more useful
if totalized by months and by days.

263. Such is the modern business method: instead of dump-
ing the raw material of transactions into a day book to be thence
digested by journalization, it is predigested by being in the first
instance distributed among specialized books of original entry.
These books build up the ledger accounts, contributing daily

details and monthly aggregates; some of them, like the cash book, *are* themselves accounts dissevered from the rest of the ledger.

264. While the two processes of analyzing the transaction into its debits and credits and of combining those of like nature were becoming facilitated by the adoption of numerous posting mediums in place of the single journal, another solution of the problem was developing; namely, the equipping of the books of original entry with additional money columns for distribution and aggregation.   This was applied in some cases to the journal which continued to be the sole posting medium, and in others to the specialized mediums which had taken over part of the functions of the journal.   Thus the simplification of the journal developed on two distinct lines: the introduction of separate and specialized books, and the introduction of separate and specialized columns.

265. Looking through the pages of any journal, it will be seen that a few accounts appear in the majority of the items.   If, then, we add an extra column for each of these often-recurring accounts and insert all other items in the ordinary columns, we may defer posting such frequent accounts till the end of the month, or as long as we please.   For a columnar journal of this type the arrangement shown in Article 249, Figure 45, where the money columns are placed on the outside and the wording in the middle, is often advantageous.   Supposing cash, merchandise, debits to expense, and credits to interest to be the frequently required postings, the arrangement might be as shown in Figure 46.

266. The word "Sundries" is here used to denote all other accounts than cash, merchandise, expense, and interest. Amounts in the Sundries columns are separately posted to the respective accounts and in order to trace them a folio column is ruled next to those columns.   At the bottom of the page the addition of each column is made and the totals carried forward to the head of the next page.   If correct, the sum of the debits will be equal to the sum of the credits.   The totals of the special

Figure 46
COLUMNAR JOURNAL

Dr. | Cr.

Exp.	Mdse.	Cash	Sun-dries	Entry	Sun-dries	Cash	Mdse.	Inter-est

columns will be posted in a lump at the end of the month, thus saving much labor and turning of leaves.

267. Besides this economy of time and space, the columnar method is useful for keeping group accounts and subordinate accounts without the formality of two grades of ledger.

For example, in discussing James Jones' balance sheet (Figure 19), we found a composite item consisting of amounts due from various personal debtors, $15,972.15. This is the aggregate of numerous individual accounts. Now if two special columns had been provided in the columnar journal and entitled (say) "Accounts Receivable, Dr.," and "Accounts Receivable, Cr.," the aggregate might be ascertained at any time from the totals of these columns by balancing; the items being also posted to the individual accounts, as noted in the folio columns.

268. To obtain the aggregate balance at the end of each month the balance at the beginning would be placed *under* the total of the debit column and then the balance struck:

FIGURE 47

	ACCOUNTS RECEIVABLE Dr.			ACCOUNTS RECEIVABLE Cr.	
[Total for month] Balance brought forward			[Total for month] Balance carried forward		

By bringing the previous balance *under* the column instead of bringing it to the top, we preserve the monthly total clear and distinct. The same device is also useful in other than columnar books.

269. More usually, however, the monthly totals are posted to a formal general ledger account, as will be explained hereafter.

270. There is danger of overdoing the principle of columnization. If we attempt to carry too many columns, the necessity of adding them up after a very few entries in each introduces a great many useless figures. In a great number of columns extending a long distance across the page there is danger also of inserting the amount in the wrong column.

271. In a multi-columnar journal there is great waste of space; for with ten columns, nine-tenths of each column, on an average, must be vacant. If we get rid of the idea that each amount must necessarily come exactly in line with its descriptive entry, we can carry a large number of accounts by the process of *side-posting*.

272. Suppose an ordinary journal with two money columns only, but occupying the left-hand pages alone, the right-hand pages being devoted to the side-posting or analysis. There are, say, thirty lines to the page. Let the right-hand page be ruled in four columns, two for the analysis of debits and two for the analysis of credits. There will then be sixty lines in which to enter the thirty possible debits, and sixty lines for the thirty possible credits, so that there will be ample room, allowing for names of accounts and for totals brought and carried forward. But the side-posting must be done one account at a time, and only when the journal page is complete. Suppose, for example, that we begin with debits to Cash. We write at the top in red the amount brought from the previous page; then passing down the journal we post every debit to Cash until we have exhausted them, checking each as we do so. When the last has been posted, we either add these debits together in red or leave a line for doing so later. Next we take up another account, say Expense, and pick out all the debits relating to that account. We shall finally have the entire contents of the journal classified into columns, but these will be solid, compact columns, not the straggling ones produced by the ordinary columnization. (See Figure 48.)

273. The loose-leaf principle may also be utilized to classify the journal while retaining its time-honored form. Each frequently recurring type of entry may be assigned to a separate page and additional pages inserted as these fill up, so that on the last day of the month it is only necessary to complete the entries by addition, they having already been posted in detail.

If, for example, the charging of interest on personal accounts is one of the normal entries regularly occurring, a loose-leaf journal page is headed:

Sundries Dr. to Interest

and each charge of that nature is entered thereon as it occurs, with uniform specifications which may be columnized to suit the requirements. The posting of the debits is kept up day by day. As the pages fill up, others are inserted and the additions made continuous to the end of the month when the compound entry is completed.

274. In this way, we have the same results as in monthly journalization, without the delay incident to that plan (Articles 258, 259). But in the rigidly bound book this would have been impracticable, as the space required for each class of entry could not be predetermined; if too much space were allowed, there would be waste; if too little, confusion and intermingling. There is an elasticity which is of great advantage in the modern method of first preparing the sheets and then binding them into books rather than binding first and then accommodating the writings to them.

275. Recurring to the direct posting mediums, or partial journals, such as cash book and sales book, it may be observed that in many kinds of business the cash book may be made to

FIGURE 48

SIDE-POSTING

[LEFT-HAND PAGE]   [RIGHT-HAND PAGE]

Date	Journal	Dr.	Cr.	Analysis of Debits	Analysis of Debits	Analysis of Credits
				Cash	Expense	
				$117.23		
				269.42		
				300.00		
				118.25		
				617.42		
				$1422.32		

contain all the entries for which the journal has been kept open, as stated in Article 251, thus completely abolishing the journal. The cash book is eligible for this office, since it is a complete account, having both sides.   A fictitious receipt of money is entered on the one side and is compensated by a fictitious payment on the other side.   Thus, in a bank which pays interest on deposits, the usual formula is:

$$\text{Interest/Depositors}$$

But this may, instead of a journal entry, be two cash book entries:

$$\text{Interest/Cash}$$
$$\text{Cash/Depositors}$$

as if the bank had *paid* the amounts of interest to the depositors and they had redeposited the same.   In fact, many banks do actually draw checks for the interest and send them to each depositor; if the depositor (as oftenest happens) sends back the check indorsed for deposit the fact in these banks coincides with the fiction in the former class.   Objection may be made to this journalization by means of a pair of cash entries, that it inflates both sides of the Cash account by the same amount.   This, however, is not considered a very great evil.   Those who are very punctilious as to keeping the cash "pure" may place the amounts of such entries outside of the Cash column to exclude them from its total, or may write them in colored ink with the same purpose.

276. Where several posting mediums are used, it will happen that there are entries which affect two of the posting mediums, for example, sales for cash, where there is no known person to be charged for the sale and to be credited for the cash.   This seems to have presented a difficulty for some writers on bookkeeping, and they have set forth two remedies.   The one is not to make any entry in the sales book at all, but to post cash sales direct to the Sales account in the ledger.   This makes the sales book an incomplete record of sales and destroys the unity of the total sales entry in the ledger. The other way is to establish an account representing the purchasers for cash, entitled, perhaps, "Cash Sales." This is debited in the usual course from the sales book and credited from the cash book.

But it seems to me that these devices are entirely useless and that no posting is needed. If we look upon the cash book as a Cash account, the debit to Cash is already made; if we look upon the sales book as a segment of the Sales account, that credit is effected. All that is necessary is to mark the cash entry and the sales entry each as the posting of the other.

277. Any "auxiliary" book may almost invariably be treated, not merely as a posting medium, but as an actual account, or half-account in detail, although there may be a more condensed account in the ledger. Especially is this view requisite when we consider postings as made from the original papers which represent transactions.

CHAPTER XVII

POSTING FROM TICKETS

278. As I have already said, in modern business the primary record of any normal transaction is made on a paper of some kind. These papers for the most part have an evidential value: they are proof of some fact and constitute *vouchers* between the concern and its subordinates or those outsiders who do business with it—the conegotiants. The latter are the more valuable, but the highest degree of value in a voucher is attained when it embodies admissions, adverse to themselves, on the part of the conegotiant in the transaction and of every subordinate who has to do with it; when everyone who is charged with value admits his responsibility, and everyone claiming value defines the extent of his claim in writing. The subject of the voucher is a most important one, especially to the auditor, and is constantly assuming greater importance. A large part of the business world is at the stage where the only vouchers recognized are those for cash paid. It is beginning, however, to be generally seen that when cash is received, some other value is given and that an acknowledgment of this other value is desirable; hence the voucher *with* cash is coming to be exacted as well as the voucher *for* cash. For example, a bank files the deposit slip which is a voucher *with* cash, as well as the checks, which are a voucher *for* cash.

279. But this is not the place for the treatment of business papers as vouchers; it is solely their use as posting tickets, irrespective of serving as evidence, with which we are now concerned.

The use of the ticket as a posting source is a modern development. Forty years ago, although the ticket existed, it was used only once; it was "written up" in the day book, or in the journal, or in the auxiliary, as the case might be, but thereafter it was dead. No posting was considered legitimate unless it was from book to book. Even the banks, having written up deposit slips, remittance letters, checks, and drafts in books called "debit cash" and "credit cash," posted the depositors' accounts from these clumsy books and not from the easily handled tickets, as is now universally done.

280. The thorough application of the voucher principle results in a paper for every transaction which occurs, even those known as journal entries. If the auditor finds such a complete set of vouchers, conveniently arranged, he can make himself independent of the books; he can arrive at results which will verify, or disprove, the results of the books far more effectually than the old plan of "ticking off" and may readily introduce a different and instructive point of view by reclassification.

281. In a thorough-going ticket system, the distinction between "writing-up" and posting vanishes and every ticket is simply entered in every place where it should be, at least twice, often more times. The state of the books is just the same as if one of the entries had been made through a posting medium. It cannot always be told afterwards which process was actually employed.

282. The ticket, or voucher, should have appropriate places for noting the fact of the postings having been made, either by a reference number or letter, or by a check mark. All tickets of a certain form may in some cases be provided with a serial number so as to determine the order of occurrence if necessary; or again, when made up from outside, such order of rotation may be denoted by a numbering or dating mechanism, to be applied as they come in.

283. The practical advantages of posting from ticket to book over posting from book to book are as follows:

1. The ticket is brought with the left hand close to the point where the entry is made so that there is no need to rely on memory even for the brief space of time it takes to pass from the page of a book to the page of another book.   This brief time is sufficient to cause many errors, from the prototype and the copy not being under the eye at the same moment.

2. The tickets may and should be assorted into an order which will go straight through the ledger without wandering back and forth.   A great part of the bookkeeper's time is wasted in the physical exercise of turning leaves.   This advantage attends also the loose-leaf systems of accounts where a regular consecution can be maintained.

3. As only one of the tickets at a time is exposed to view, the eye does not so easily lead to error by falling upon a wrong amount.

4. Tickets can be distributed and several bookkeepers work on them at the same time; whereas with a bound book one must wait for another.

284. The keeping of the tickets after use requires consideration and it is important to instal a good filing system.   The simplest is to file by date, and this will do where reference is seldom required.   It may be in packages, in envelopes, in scrap books or vertically in drawers or boxes, tickets of the same model being, of course, kept together.   Either of these plans may also be used when the assorting is done by accounts.   An ingenious combination of posting and filing is where the account is kept, instead of a card, on an envelope in which are filed the vouchers, these being of the kind which are returned to the debtor on payment.   This plan is used in clubs, where the members' tickets for supplies go inside the envelope and the account on the outside.   When the bill is rendered, nothing more goes in or on that envelope.   When paid, it is returned, with contents, to the member, a new one being started.

285. When the vouchers are filed by dates in a monthly bundle, a cover, or jacket, may be used, having on its outside a summary or a journalization of the contents, making a posting ticket for the general ledger. Inside may be a detailed list of the vouchers for the use of any auditing authority.

286. Some vouchers, used as posting tickets, have ultimately to be past on as vouchers to someone else, like the club tickets mentioned above. In this case a duplicate is often retained for permanent record and reference; and if this can be in facsimile, as by the carbon or copying press methods, it is all the better.

287. The preserving of the original or duplicate tickets often renders it unnecessary to make any detailed entry in the books, but simply the amount. Thus, it was formerly customary to copy each bill of goods sent out into the sales book; but the more modern practice is to enter there and in the purchaser's account merely the total sold, without specification of items or prices. Again, the totaling of the sales themselves is rapidly performed by listing them on one of the modern adding machines which give an automatic total. If the machine has the additional feature of combining with the adder a typewriter for the names, the basic accounts (those represented by posting mediums) are, in the loose-leaf methods, entirely posted by machine.

CHAPTER XVIII

THE LEDGER

288. Having treated of the nature of accounts, their construction, classification, relation, and interdependence, it remains to speak of them as an organized system or ledger, which when complete is capable of recording all the occurrences within a given sphere of proprietorship.

289. The ledger is sometimes incomplete, and is then frequently known as a "single-entry" ledger. This means that a part of the accounts are omitted or neglected, so that many entries are only half-posted. Usually it is the proprietary and economic accounts, or some of them, which are suppressed. The missing accounts are implied in the transactions, and when an accountant examines such a system he invariably constructs the lacking accounts as the easiest way out; which rather indicates that their omission did not save any labor in the end.

290. We must not hastily assume that a ledger is incomplete, because the missing accounts do not appear between the same covers as the others. It is very probably the case that in some other book or on some sheet of paper, perhaps in untechnical form, these accounts lie hidden, for they certainly exist implicitly if not explicitly. It is not the insertion of the words, "Dr. to" and "Cr. by," which makes the account; and it is not the binding which limits the ledger; a ledger may be contained in a dozen volumes, or a dozen ledgers may be contained in one volume; or

there may be no binding at all, as in the card ledger; or there may be a removable binding, as in the loose-leaf ledger. The relation of the accounts to each other, or to some other account to which they refer, is what determines the extent of the ledger.

291. The accounts which appear in the balance sheet may be group accounts (Article 74), in which case there are necessarily accounts of a lower grade for each member of a certain group; or, in a limited sphere, without the use of any group accounts, each account may enter directly into the balance sheet. The difference between these two modes of presentation is analogous to the difference between a town meeting where each voter participates, and a representative assembly. The case where the accounts are all of one grade, may be called a *simple* ledger. This is frequent in small business spheres, but infrequent in the large ones.

292. When there are several grades of accounts, there are a principal ledger and subordinate ledgers; or as often called, a "general" ledger and special ledgers. The former is always complete, but the latter may or may not be complete, or self-balancing. Taking for example a mortgage ledger, such as described in Article 74, all its balances are on the debit side and it would seem impossible to make a trial balance. It is true that the trial balance is one-sided, but the figures with which this should agree are elsewhere; they are the balance of the group account, Mortgages, in the general ledger.

293. In order to make the debits and credits of the special ledger equal, there is sometimes introduced into it what is called a "controlling account," which is usually entitled "General Ledger." It is exactly the reverse of the Mortgages account in the general ledger; what is debited there is credited here and vice versa. It certainly puts the mortgage ledger "in balance," if that is considered desirable.

294. It might be urged that this controlling account is illogical, inasmuch as increase of the asset, "mortgages," must invariably be represented by a debit. But when we look more closely we see that the controlling account is proprietary in its nature; that it represents one section of the proprietorship. It might be headed "The Proprietor in account with Mortgage Debtors." From this point of view it is correct in theory and its balance ought to appear, as it does, to the credit.

295. The controlling account is not, however, so much a necessity as a convenience. It is quite easy to dispense with it and to check the total of the mortgage ledger by the balance of the group account in the general ledger. It is not necessary that a trial balance or a balance sheet should always be two-sided when, as in this case and the case cited in Article 123, there are no negative or subtractive values.

296. The choice between incorporating a controlling account into the subordinate ledger, and considering it controlled by the corresponding account in the general ledger, depends in each system upon the answer to this question: Is it preferable to give the keeper of the subordinate ledger a chance to prove his own accuracy or to have him report his total to the keeper of the general ledger for verification? The decision will depend on personal and administrative considerations having no relation to the theory of accounts; theoretically either procedure is correct.

297. In a system of accounts of moderate extent, a general ledger and subordinate ledgers may be kept in the same volume by the use of one of the loose-leaf plans, thus avoiding expense and the appearance of complexity.

298. It is simply a question of using two colors of paper in providing the ledger sheets. For example, if the detailed accounts are in blue paper, let a smaller supply of sheets of exactly the same ruling be in buff. Buff will then indicate the general ledger accounts, that is, those which are directly tributary to the balance sheet either because they represent units which need no subdivision or because they represent groups. The blue pages represent the members of groups; just before each group of blue pages comes a buff page which summarizes the figures of the blue pages.

The little balance sheet of Jones & Smith (Article 93) when expanded into a ledger combining both general and subordinate accounts, might be contained in the following leaves:

A buff leaf for a summary account of Cash.
　　Blue leaves as required for details of cash transactions; cash book.
A buff leaf for a Merchandise (asset) account.
　　Blue leaves constituting invoice book.
A buff leaf for a Sales account.
　　Blue leaves constituting sales book.
A buff leaf for a group account for Bills Receivable.
　　Blue leaves constituting bill book for receivables.
A buff leaf for a group account for Customers.
　　Blue leaves containing individual accounts, with customers alphabetically arranged; the customers ledger.
A buff leaf for the Real Estate account (a single piece).
A buff leaf for Bills Payable account.
　　Blue leaves constituting bill book.
A buff leaf for a group account for Creditors.
　　Blue leaves of individual creditors, alphabetically arranged; "the bought ledger."
A buff leaf for account of the Mortgage.
A buff leaf for Capital account.
　　Blue leaves for partners' accounts.
A buff leaf for Profit and Loss.
　　Blue leaves for various economic accounts.

299. Thus nearly all the records of a moderate business may be contained in a single binder and a transfer holder of precisely the same arrangement, with the advantages of two grades of ledger, general and subordinate, giving both comprehensive and minute information. Blue leaves are inserted as needed, and removed when filled. Buff leaves may be kept separately when removed, forming a condensed history of the business.

300. If the accounts are sufficiently numerous to divide into two or more volumes, the personal accounts, debtor and creditor,

should be in a different volume from that containing the accounts used as *posting mediums* (Chapter XVI) as, in posting from book to book, both books should be open. With the ticket system (Chapter XVII) this precaution is unnecessary. Even if a single volume is used, the leaves of posting mediums may be temporarily detached while posting.

301. Probably the most adaptable ruling for a combination ledger is the three-column or balance ledger (Figure 7). If a part of the leaves be delivered without ruled down lines, special rulings may be made by hand to suit special forms of account. This would be almost impracticable with a bound book.

302. Postings to the general ledger consist of the totals, usually monthly, of the basic accounts, such as Cash, Purchases, and Sales. The trial balance of the general ledger should be first verified, which, from the small number of its accounts, is easily done. Then each subordinate ledger has its own trial balance, verified by its controlling account or by the balance of the corresponding general ledger account.

303. The ledger may be considered as *the* book of account; all others are tributary to it or derived from it, or are sections of it, kept apart for convenience. The modern tendency in accounting practice is that the complete cycle of accounts as embodied periodically in the balance sheet or equation of status shall be the basis of all records; that there be no auxiliary books independent of the ledger accounts but that each shall definitely and regularly prepare materials for those accounts.

304. Such of the accounts as are confidential and not intended to be accessible to the office force are sometimes kept in a private ledger. These accounts are most frequently, in firms, those of the partners and of such investments as it is unnecessary to have appear in the current accounts, the scope of the private ledger being governed by circumstances. If it is intended to conceal the amount of capital, it is desirable to keep in the private ledger, besides the proprietary accounts, some specific ones. For example, in the accounts of Jones & Smith (Figure 23) it may be thought best to keep confidential the valuation of the real estate, the amount of the mortgage, and the capital of each partner. The private ledger would then contain the following accounts:

Real Estate..............................	$10,000.00	
Mortgage Payable...........................		$4,000.00
Jones.......................................		47,645.62
Smith.......................................		23,822.81
Balance of Private Ledger......................	*65,468.43*	
	$75,468.43	$75,468.43

This balance, $65,468.43, would need to be furnished to the general ledger bookkeeper before he could verify his trial balance, which would take this form:

Cash..	$8,589.08	
Merchandise.................................	39,249.38	
Bills Receivable.............................	7,000.00	
Personal Debtors............................	24,095.32	
Personal Creditors...........................		$5,465.35
Bills Payable...............................		8,000.00
Private Ledger...............................		*65,468.43*
	$78,933.78	$78,933.78

305. Where the number of accounts in the general ledger is small and the transactions are of a few types, the ledger may take the tabular form, which is self-proving because the additions and subtractions operate both transversely and vertically.

306. The modes in which the ledger may be tabulated are so various that it is difficult to give a typical illustration; but Figure 49 may be suggestive.

307. Taking the same list of accounts shown in Article 304, a ledger is to be constructed which shall show each month all the transactions of the month, with the results at the close. Entries bearing the same letter form a complete transaction, as will be seen by collating them. The economic accounts are kept in a separate table and are not balanced but aggregated from month

FIGURE 49
TABULAR GENERAL LEDGER

Balances, 1st Dr.	Balances, 1st Cr.	Dr.	Transactions, Month of............ Specific Accounts	Cr.	Balances, 31st Dr.	Balances, 31st Cr.
$13,675.23		$16,713.90	(a) Cash............(b)	$20,240.84	$10,148.29	
24,635.84		14,416.80	(c) Merchandise (at cost)............(d)	15,618.79	23,433.85	
4,236.79		1,000.00	(e) Bills Receivable............(a)	1,247.92	3,988.87	
12,793.64		19,519.74	(d) Personal Debtors............(a)	15,465.98	15,847.40	
			(e)	1,000.00		
	$6,000.00	3,000.00	(b) Bills Payable............(f)	2,000.00		$5,000.00
	7,618.25	14,319.74	(b) Personal Creditors............(c)	14,416.80		5,715.31
		2,000.00	(f)			
	3,675.19		*Economic Accounts*............	1,279.85		4,955.04
38,048.06		300.00	(b) *Private Ledger*............			37,748.06
$55,341.50 (Totals Brought Forward)	**$55,341.50**	**$71,270.18**		**$71,270.18**	**$53,418.41**	**$53,418.41** (Totals Carried Forward)

Balances, 1st Dr.	Balances, 1st Cr.	Dr.	Economic Accounts	Cr.	Carried Forward Dr.	Carried Forward Cr.
$2,000.00	$8,882.35	$1,000.00	(d) Profit on Sales............	$3,900.95		$12,783.30
3,000.00		1,500.00	(b) Rent............		$3,000.00	
152.16		.93.18	(b) Salaries............		4,500.00	
55.00		27.92	(b) Freight............		245.34	
3,675.19		1,279.85	(b) Interest............		82.92	
			Balance............		4,955.04	
$8,882.35 (Totals Brought Forward)	**$8,882.35**	**$3,900.95**		**$3,900.95**	**$12,783.30**	**$12,783.30**

Key to Transactions: (a) Cash. receipts, (b) Cash payments, (c) Purchases, (d) Sales, (e) Notes accepted, (f) Notes given.

to month.   Their resultant, however, is carried into the table of the special accounts.   The private ledger plan is also illustrated.

For any incidental transaction of a type not comprised in the key, a letter is assigned and the explanation given in manuscript.

CHAPTER XIX

PRECAUTIONS AGAINST ERROR

308. Experience shows that the intellect, even in so mechanical a process as posting, cannot be absolutely relied on to be free from error. Error or omission will occur in a small percentage of the work and is usually caused by inattention. This is either temperamental, or else accidental, resulting from interruption, disturbance, fatigue from too long-continued work or illness. The errors thus caused would be found by the next trial balance; but in the meantime the inaccuracy of the account might bring about a loss. To avoid such loss and also to minimize the labor of the trial balance, various plans are in use for a daily check on the current work.

309. This check will be the more efficacious according as it is independent of, and different from, the original work. If we take exactly the same road as before we are most likely to strike the same pitfalls. The same aberration of the intellect which caused an error will be apt to produce the like again.

310. Different minds find different means the best in this respect, and each should seek the check which he h'mself finds efficacious. The quantity of work to be gone over is also a determinant, as a long-continued series of postings has a benumbing effect so that a very simple test may fail, from that proneness to assent which everyone feels in greater or less degree.

311. Misposting will hardly ever pass unnoticed if before leaving each posting, by a conscious effort of will, one wakes himself up to the real meaning of what he is recording and, shutting out all other thoughts, asks himself, "Is this true?" This habit is a valuable one to form.

312. The simplest check is to go over all the postings a second time, comparing with the original.   To show, in case of interruption, how far the process has gone, a check mark ($\checkmark$) is placed opposite each item *after* it is found correct.   These ticks should not be too large, but contained within the ruled lines; an unticked line is a danger signal which may be obscured by a large tick.   If an item has been posted to the wrong account, the true account will be blank; the posting must be supplied and ticked. If the item had been altogether omitted, the matter is at an end; if it had been posted in a wrong place, there is somewhere in the books a line without a tick, which when observed must be instantly investigated.

313. If another person, not the original poster, conducts the comparison and ticking there is some additional security, for the new man comes with a fresh eye to the work.

314. When assistance is available, it is quite usual to work in a team of two, in the process called "calling back," "calling off," or "calling over."   One person reads off the name or number of an account and the other, turning to the proper page, responds with the figures.   I am aware that this method is used by many public accountants in auditing, probably to save time, the bound-book system not allowing of any other division of labor. Yet I believe that two persons working separately will accomplish more, and more surely, than in the "calling-off" process. The ear is less reliable than the eye and more easily deceived.   The tasks of the two men are not precisely equal: the one being comparatively inactive, and therefore a large part of his time being wasted, while his mind becomes torpid through inaction and when, after hundreds of correct postings, an incorrect one is called off he fails to observe it.   If it is possible to subdivide the work so that each can check a separate part by eye, I think it will be found that the two will accomplish more and better, separately, than together.

315. Quite a different class of check systems is composed of those where we reconstruct the accounts anew from the original sources, or by the converse process reconstruct the posting sources anew from the accounts.   The resulting lists are compared in total with their prototypes, hence the final test embraces but few figures and the chance of "assenting" to an error is greatly lessened; while the relation of the figures is altered into new combinations.

316. A check ledger or balance ledger is in effect a duplicate ledger kept in some simpler and briefer, perhaps rougher, way, because it is not needed for precise information but for the purpose of a check on the ordinary ledger.   For this reason, it may be kept in pencil, dates may be omitted and all descriptive matter, a large number of accounts may appear at one opening, or it may carry balances only and not transactions.   This may be a very good plan in a mercantile business where balances are not very often called for except monthly.   It serves mainly as a corrective of the monthly trial balance, all final balances being compared before totaling.

317. In a banking business of any kind, the correct keeping of depositors' accounts is a matter of the greatest importance.   The balance should be at all times ascertainable and reliable to avoid the risk of overpayment.   The balance ledger was therefore introduced as a check on the ordinary ledger.   Its peculiarity is that each account runs horizontally, occupying a line across the page. The first column in the page contains the initial balances, usually in red, of thirty or forty accounts, a name on each line.   When totaled and aggregated this column is a trial balance of the deposit system.   The next column contains all the credits for the day on each account, a third column all the debits, and the fourth

the resulting balances of the next day. It is evident that the totals may be proved, forming the equation:

Old Balance + Credits − Debits = New Balance

FIGURE 50

THE BANK BALANCE LEDGER

Names	Balances Jan. 15	Credits	Debits	Balances Jan. 16	Credits	Debits
A B	1734.16	223.19	100.00	1857.35		
B B	2000.00	300.00	463.17	1836.83		
C B	2217.65	500.00		2717.65		
Totals	5951.81	1023.19	563.17	6411.83		

318. This is the general principle on which it is worked, omitting a number of details and variations in practice, such as providing for debits in detail, writing the daily credits in the same column as the balances but in different ink, placing inactive accounts by themselves, providing for overdrafts (debit balances), making part of the pages narrower so that the names do not have to be rewritten.

319. The convenience and advantages of the balance ledger are so great that in most banks it has become the principal ledger, and the "vertical" accounts have been disused altogether. The check on it is the monthly statement which is written up day by day with a facsimile copy, and which gives debits and credits in detail. In this point of view the balance ledger might properly have been treated in a later chapter.

320. Directly contrary to the methods which duplicate the ledger are those processes which are known under the title of "reverse posting." I think I was the originator of this name, at least, though the process itself was doubtless thought out by others before me.

9

321. The essential feature of reverse posting is to reconstruct from the ledger itself the sources of the ledger, or if the posting is from tickets to reconstruct a few of the accounts from the many. These few which are to be rebuilt are those which enter into the majority of all the regular transactions—those which would be selected for the basis of posting mediums if ticket posting were not employed.

322. Supposing that the debits were normally for Cash, Sales, and Interest and that the credits were usually for Cash, Purchases, Discounts, and Expense, a small sheet is ruled with a column for each of these basic accounts and an extra one for Sundries or miscellaneous.

FIGURE 51

REVERSE POSTING SHEET.................19...   Dr.

	Cash	Sales	Interest	Sundries
17 96 98				

REVERSE POSTING SHEET.............19...   Cr.

Cash	Purchases	Discount	Expense	Sundries

323. These forms may be on a single page, or on opposite pages of the same leaf, or on separate leaves.

324. The columns are to be filled strictly by copying what is found in the account and the proof is made by adding each

column.   Each column will correspond in its total to the total of
the transactions of one of the posting mediums or one of the basic
accounts.   The two Sundries columns will be equal in aggregate.

325. It might be recommended (though I have not seen this
in practice) to make the totals *continuous* during the month,
carrying forward the totals from the bottom of one sheet to the
top of the next.   The totals of the posting medium added in
pencil to the same point would always be proved.   The same
result might be attained by recapitulating the daily totals of
columns on a monthly sheet, and aggregating these day by day.

326. An important question in the use of reverse posting is:
When shall the sheet be filled? at the time of posting, or as a
distinct processs?   It is easier to insert the posting in the reverse
sheet while the page lies open before you.   Many do this, keeping
the sheet alongside and as soon as each entry is made in the
ledger transcribing it on the sheet.   The entire efficacy of the
reverse posting process depends on the contents of the sheet being
a transcript from the ledger, right or wrong, and from nowhere
else.   I should myself be afraid that, with the memory and sight
of the original so freshly before me, I might revert to it and write
it instead of the erroneous ledger sum which I ought to copy, and
which I should thus fail to detect.

327. The alternative method is, first, to go through with all
the posting; when the last entry is posted, and not before, to take
up the reverse sheet and fill it from the ledger.   This again has
two alternatives:

1. To examine every account in the ledger for transactions of
this date.
2. To leave, on posting, some indication or trail by which the
accounts affected may alone be considered and all those
which are untouched may be disregarded.

328. Plan (1) would be a very thorough one where the accounts are few but active, so that the majority of them had some

change each day.   It would eliminate some classes of errors such as posting the same item in two different places.

329. Plan (2) may be carried out in either of several different ways.   One is to use strips of paper at the time of posting, inserting them so that they project above the page where the posting occurs.   Then in the reverse process these are used as markers, and only those pages are referred to where a marker is found.   There is a modification consisting in a variation in the color of the strip, using, for example, red strips for debits and black strips for credits.   I think this dangerous, because it suggests too much.   Perhaps a debit has been erroneously posted to the credit side, but the red strip suggests a debit and the reverse posting is made to the debit sheet; then the error is concealed instead of being revealed.   I should decidedly prefer a strip which would merely indicate the page and leave the reverse poster to do his work without suggestion.   There is an objection to this slip plan, that a posting to the wrong page might be undiscovered. In the card ledger no strips need be used, but each card to which posting has been made left a little higher than the others or a little to one side.

330. Another way of "blazing the trail" is to prepare the reverse posting sheet by writing in each column in advance the numbers of the pages affected, taking these numbers from the original sources.   In Figure 52 in the Cash column I have indicated the place of these numbers.   This would discover such an error as alluded to in the previous paragraph unless the original source were improperly folioed.

331. As an extension of the method in Article 330, the names as well as the folios may be included in the proof of the posting. It is recommended that only a few letters of the name be written in the preparatory work and that, at the time of the reverse posting, the remaining letters be filled in.   This compels the attention to be fixed upon the name, which might otherwise be overlooked.

FIGURE 52

REVERSE POSTING SHEET

Dr. / Cr.

Sundries	Interest	Sales	Cash	No.	Name	Cash	Purchases	Discount	Expense	Sundries
			200	22	Smith		179.63			
				56	Jones	180				
				73	Sullivan					
				109	Tho					
				126	Fit					

332. When tickets are used for posting, or for making up the posting mediums, a most advantageous way of preparing the sheets is to assort all the tickets in a single series, alphabetically or numerically, so as to bring them into the same order as the pages of the ledger and to avoid the waste of time through turning back and forward. To give the fullest effect to the verification the number or name of the account should be in the middle of the sheet and the columns to the left and right.

333. The highest degree of certitude is reached when the verification or reverse posting is done not by the original poster, but by another, who has no prepossessions as to the transaction. He turns to the account and transcribes literally what is found there. He is compelled to look at the name, the amount, which side it is on, and what its source; none of these facts are suggested to him. If, then, after he has reversed every posting the columns of his sheet exactly agree in total with the total given elsewhere, the evidence is very strong that all the posting is correct.

334. In a savings bank, where the accounts are very numerous and the current entries are all cash, this method with various modifications is used extensively and effectually. In the larger institutions of the kind it is further found advisable to "sectionize" the ledgers; that is, to divide the whole mass of accounts into large blocks, say of 2,000 or 3,000 accounts bearing consecutive numbers. This feature is carried into the daily work by making a break in the list at the end of each section or block. This presupposes that each teller has made a list, either by mechanism or with a pen, of the tickets, the total agreeing with the state of the cash and forming the standard to which the reverse posting must conform, if correct.

335. An account must be kept with each of the blocks of accounts constituting a section. This makes an intermediate system between the general ledger account of Depositors, and the individual account of each depositor. This will give information

at the time of the trial balance as to how much the balances of each section *ought* to produce. If some of them are found correct, the attention is concentrated upon those which show differences. This principle of sectionizing is of great value in all cases where there is a large number of accounts to be handled—so large that the search for an error is very laborious, like the hunting for needles in a haystack. If we divide the haystack into a number of smaller stacks, in many of which it is apparent that there is no needle, the search is much facilitated.

336. Returning to the reverse sheet for testing transactions in savings banks, we have assumed that a consecutive list of transactions has been prepared at the teller's desk, by which he proves his cash and to which the bookkeeper's sheet must finally conform, the latter being numerically arranged and broken into sections. These two lists are sometimes combined in what is known as the "coupon" method. This consists in keeping at the teller's desk a set of sheets, one for each section and entering on these, preferably from the pass book, each transaction which has been made. The transactions thus assort themselves instead of being assorted afterwards. The sheets are in a peculiar form, there being two money columns with a perforation between, with spaces for number and name.

The first of the money columns is left blank by the teller, who uses only the outer one. He balances his cash by this outer column, aggregating all the sheets, tears off the strip or coupon and retains it. The remainder goes to the bookkeeping department as a reverse sheet. It is not quite so convenient for that purpose as a consecutive list in numeric order, for the accounts in a heavy section have to be picked out of a mass, or else there is much turning of leaves. On the other hand, if the section fails to prove, it is very easy to discover the error by laying the coupon in the place where it originally was and comparing the amounts as they stand side by side. There is no exact chronological list and no exact numeric list.

FIGURE 53

PROVING SHEET			COUPON
12 Apr. 1907 Section 23 460,001—465,000			23
No.	Name	Deposits	12 Apr. 07
462,749	Smith		100
460,979	Jones		25
463,652	Robinson		63
464,998	Murphy		17
460,723	Becker		3
	&c.		

337. Where the "three-column" ledger (debits, credits, and balance) is used, it is very important to have the Balance column verified; more important, in fact, than the debit and credit columns, for the Balance column is relied upon as a guide for instant payments. There are two ways of insuring the accuracy of the balances, which may be termed the "double balance" and the "balance posting" methods. The former requires the addition to the sheets (Figure 52 or 53) of two columns for Old Balance and New Balance. Figure 53 would then be arranged as follows:

No.	Name	Old Balance	New Balance	Deposits	Deposits
462,749	Smith	2769.13	2869.13	100.00	100.00

The teller has inserted only

462,749	Smi				100.00

and the testing clerk has added

	th	2769.13	2869.13	100.00	

all copied from the ledger. Thus an error in balancing would be as certain of detection as an error in posting; for the difference between the totals of the Old Balance column and of the New Balance column must be equal to the totals of the deposits (or drafts).

"Balance posting" equally insures correctness of balances with much less labor. Its essential feature is working *backward* from the balance (which is first to be entered) to the transaction which is inferred from the increase or decrease exhibited in the Balance column. No change is made in the sheets, whether of Figure 52 or 53, but the variation is in the order of posting the ledger. Thus if the ledger account of John Smith stands as follows:

462,749
JOHN SMITH

Date	Dr.	Cr.	Balance
1907	Brought forward		2769.13

and it is desired to post a deposit of $100, the posting and proving are done in the following stages:

First Operation. Taking the deposit ticket, the bookkeeper writes the date and then, instead of entering the $100 to the credit, he enters in the Balance column, 2,869.13, and nothing else. Continuing this process until all the accounts having transactions have been rebalanced, he turns over the tickets to the head bookkeeper. Smith's account then reads:

1907	Brought forward		2769.13
April 12			2869.13

Second Operation. Another bookkeeper having no intimation of the transaction *infers* from the increased balance that it was a deposit of $100, and inserts that sum in the credit column of the ledger:

1907	Brought forward		2769.13
April 12		100.00	2869.13

This is exactly the same entry as would appear if the entry had been made first and the rebalancing done afterward; but there is this important difference, that an error in striking the balance would cause the $100 to vary from the original ticket and lead to detection.

Third Operation. The $100, which, if the balancing has been correctly done, represents the correct transaction, is copied into the sheet opposite the proper number and name, and the sheets delivered to the head bookkeeper.

Fourth Operation. The tickets and the sheets, reaching the head bookkeeper by different channels, are compared by him. If he finds that they agree in all respects, he is assured not only that the debits and credits are correct and on the right sides but, what is still more important, the balances are reliable. He may, however, have overlooked some discrepancy, or some transaction may have been omitted altogether; hence a still further proof is made.

Fifth Operation. The columns of debits and credits are added up by sheets and sections and aggregated; and if the totals agree exactly with those of the actual cash received and paid, there is the highest degree of assurance that all the work, including the balancing, has been correctly done. Experience shows that it is almost impossible for an error to evade the process.

338. There is another class of precautionary methods, which consist in transcribing, not the figures themselves, but a so-called "check number" derived from the digits of the amount of the transaction through the properties of 9 or some other number. I shall not discuss these, as they are somewhat outside of the province of accountancy.

CHAPTER XX

THE DETECTION OF ERRORS

CLASSIFICATION OF ERRORS—SELECTION OF PROCEDURE—TRANSPOSITION INDICATED BY 9'S—CORRECTION OF ERROR—NARROWING THE FIELD—TABULATION OF LEDGER

339. The trial balance has been drawn off and added, and the totals of the debit and of the credit sides do not agree with each other. There is error somewhere; we ascertain the exact amount of the discrepancy (commonly called the "difference") and the pressing need is to find and remove its causes. It may be caused:

1. By a single error.
2. By several errors on the same side.
3. By an error or errors on each side.

The difference is the resultant of all these errors. They may be classed as:

4. Omission to post.
5. Duplicate posting of the same item.
6. Posting on the wrong side.
7. Substitution of one figure for another.
8. Transposition of figures.
9. Incorrect combinations of figures by addition or subtraction.

340. The selection of a procedure for exactly locating the difference will depend somewhat on the extent and multiplicity of the transactions, on the correlation of the accounts, and on the habitual accuracy of the poster. If he is known to be very accurate, so much so that his trial balance seldom shows a difference, the probability is strongly in favor of there being only one error.

On this hypothesis, we should endeavor to find an item of exactly the same amount as the difference, and ascertain if (4) or (5) has not occurred; or an item of half the amount of the difference, for (6), being a double error, doubles the difference by increasing the one side and diminishing the other. If the difference is one expressed by a single digit, it is very likely caused by (7) or (9). If (8) has occurred and is the only source of error, the difference will always be exactly divisible by 9. According to a well-known arithmetical principle, the divisibility of a number by 9 is easily ascertained without actually performing the division; simply adding the digits themselves as if they were all in the units column. 27 is divisible by 9, and 2 + 7 = 9. 13,579 is not exactly divisible by 9, for 1 + 3 + 5 + 7 + 9 = 25, and 2 + 5 = 7. Seven will be the remainder after dividing 13,579 by 9, hence a difference of $135.79 could not be caused by transposition alone. 179,865,342 is divisible by 9, because:

$$1 + 7 + 9 + 8 + 6 + 5 + 3 + 4 + 2 = 45 \text{ and } 4 + 5 = 9$$

There is nothing very wonderful in this peculiarity of 9, for it simply means that 9 is the difference between a unit of any denomination and a unit of the next denomination. If we transpose 43 into 34, we have substituted:

4 units for 4 tens, difference 4 nines
3 tens for 3 units, difference 3 nines

Every possible shifting of places results in some number of nines.

But there are many other ways of producing a nine difference than by transposition and the time expended in searching for transposible figures is frequently wasted.

A more thorough and systematic method is needed, and to adopt some such plan will generally prove a saving of time.

341. The methods for conducting a search are analogous to those described in Chapter XIX for the prevention of error. The postings may be all gone over again and checked; if already checked in advance, a distinctive mark should be adopted for the second operation. "Calling-off" may be resorted to without the dangers, referred to in Article 3 14, for the fact that there is actually something to find will keep the senses more alert than where the operation may prove useless. Then, to guard against (9) all additions and carryings forward must be re-examined and finally the making-up of the trial balance itself, for there have been cases where the ledger was absolutely correct but was misrepresented in the trial balance.

342. The foregoing procedure ought to discover errors which when corrected will bring the ledger into equilibrium. Each error when found should be rectified thoroughly, and it is very important that this should be done in proper order. Do not make the alteration in the trial balance first and the ledger afterwards, for there is then a possibility of omitting to change the ledger, and a more dangerous state of things exists: a ledger which is erroneous but apparently has the guaranty of a trial balance. Make a rigid rule to correct errors first at the source, and follow up the correction in the natural order till it reaches the total of the trial balance. It is an unwise plan, when a part of the difference is found, to subtract it from or add it to the original difference. The better way is to eliminate the old difference altogether and ascertain afresh the amount of discrepancy. Remember that the sole object of the search is to rectify the accounts, not to rectify the trial balance.

343. But it sometimes happens that after all this labor of going over the work a second time, a discrepancy still appears. The error is perhaps right on the surface, yet it is unnoticed the second time as it was the first. This is very discouraging and there is no reason to believe that a second or a third performance of the same process will be any more successful. The defect of the method is that it does not narrow down the field and gradually "corner" the error in some limited area. A method which does this must ultimately succeed, for the area diminishes until it embraces only the erroneous entry.

344. A first narrowing of the field may take place by ascertaining whether the debit or the credit side is faulty. If the trial balance is composed of totals, and not merely of balances (Article 220), we can ascertain what the grand total of each side *ought* to be, by summing the original sources. Take first the simple case of full journalization, where every entry in the ledger must have proceeded from the journal; where the contents of the ledger are merely the contents of the journal rearranged. The total of the journal is a standard for the total of the ledger, and either side which varies from that standard is erroneous.

Thus, if we have the following results:

Total of trial balance.........	$117,648.29	$117,395.74
Total of journal..............	117,648.29	117,648.29

it would be waste of time to look for error in the debit side: it must be in the credit. Of course, in practice, allowances may have to be made for accounts ruled off, etc., but this can easily be done. It may be that both sides are erroneous and then we have not gained very much. If one side is excessive and the other deficient, there is strong indication of posting to the wrong side, especially if the redundance and the shortage are equal in amount.

345. The same principles may be applied where the place of the journal has been taken by other posting mediums (Chapter XVI). The amounts contributed by each posting medium to each side are set down and their totals determined the standard to which the ledger, represented in the trial balance, ought to conform. Thus:

Debits from Cash Book......................	$..........
from Sales Book......................	....
total of Invoice Book..................	....
from Journal........................	....
Previous balances.....................	....
	$..........
less accounts closed...................	....
Total........................	$..........

Credits from Cash Book....................... $..........
........from Invoice Book.....................   ....
........total of Sales Book...................   ....
........from Journal..........................   ....
........Previous balances.....................   ....

                                              $..........
less accounts closed...................   ....

............Total........................ $..........

346. The surest way for completely tracking all errors by an exhaustive process is to *tabulate* the ledger. This process is called by some writers "analyzing," but it seems to me that "tabulation" more exactly describes it. It consists in reducing the entries in each account to the form of a horizontal line very much, in principle, like the bank balance ledger described in Article 317, or the general ledger in Article 307. In the tabulated ledger, however, as both debit and credit balances are comprised, it is necessary to allow more columns. It is governed by this equation:

Old debit balance + debit entries + new credit balance
= old credit balance + credit entries + new debit balances

The left-hand side of this equation is represented by the left-hand page of a book ruled in a number of columns, and the right-hand side by its right-hand page. The debit entries occupy a number of columns according to their sources in the various posting mediums or the basic accounts, exactly as in the reverse posting sheet (Article 331, Figure 52), and the credit entries are classified in the same way.

347. The arrangement of the tabulation might be as in Figure 54, it being supposed that the debit postings are all from a cash book, a sales book, and a journal, and the credits from cash book, invoice book, and journal.

348. Having provided these columns, it is obvious that the contents of any account may be "strung out" across the page and that, including the initial and final balances, exactly the same total will appear on each line.

FIGURE 54

TABULATION OF LEDGER

1	2	3	4	5	6		7	8	9	10	11
		(LEFT-HAND PAGE)						(RIGHT-HAND PAGE)			
Accounts	Old Balance Dr.	Debits from			New Balance Cr.		Old Balance Cr.	Credits from			New Balance Dr.
		Cash	Sales	Jour.				Cash	Invoice	Journal	

Thus, suppose that a customer, John Smith, owed at the previous trial balance $279.43; that he purchased several bills, posted from the sales book, amounting to $265.67; that he was charged by journal entry with a sum of $24.38; that he was credited "by cash" $200; and that therefore he owes at this balancing time a balance of $369.48. Entries would then appear in columns 1, 2, 4, 5, 8, and 11, as follows:

Column	1 John Smith [or folio]	
	2 Old Balance Dr......................	$279.43
	4 Debits from Sales....................	265.67
	5 Debits from Journal..................	24.38
		$569.48
	8 Credits from Cash....................	$200.00
	11 New Balance Dr.....................	369.48
		$569.48

Only two of the Balance columns can possibly be required in any given account.

349. Having entered these figures, they should be immediately added across on each page, and as the total of each is $569.48, the conclusion is that the account is correctly balanced, though nothing is yet known as to the correctness of the postings. Consistency with itself, not conformity to its prototypes, is all that is demonstrated of the ledger. But frequently the entire error is discovered during the process, not having been caused by erroneous posting, but by erroneous combination of correct entries (class 9, Article 339).

At the bottom of the page each column is added and it is evident that as every line was in equation, so the aggregates must also obey the law:

Old debit balances + debits from Cash + debits from Sales + debits from Journal + new credit balances = old credit balances + credits from Cash + credits from Invoices + credits from Journal + new debit balances.

If this does not hold good, something is wrong either with the total of some column or with the balancing of some line and this must be discovered before passing to the next page. In an obstinate case, an intermediate footing may be made about half-way down the page and this again tested by the equation. If this aggregate stands the test, the error is in the lower part of the page; if it fails, the error is above it. Thus by subdivision the error must ultimately be located and corrected.

It is recommended that the totals of each page be carried forward to the next, insuring that no unbalanced line or page has been left behind.

350. It may be thought best not to group all the entries of a certain kind into a single line, but set them down in detail, using as many lines as necessary. In the example in Article 348, the debits from Sales, $265.67, may be 4 items; $82.65, $25.33, $91.25, and $66.44. Then the account as tabulated will occupy four lines in depth instead of one.

Column 1	2	4	5	8	11
John Smith........... 279.43		82.65	24.38	200	369.48
		25.33			
		91.25			
		66.44			
Tobias Smollett	etc.				

This makes the cross-addition a little more difficult, but, as fewer accounts can be entered on a page, the cross-addition of each line may be omitted till the bottom and then the entire page be proved as a whole.

351. Accounts like Cash and Merchandise, or what we have been calling "basic" accounts, must be left to the last. Everything else is added up and probably without going any further the error will stand revealed. Column 3 should tally with the total of cash paid, or there is error there; column 4 with the total of sales, column 8 with the total of cash received, column 9 with the total of purchases, and a discrepancy in either of these totals must be traced by checking of the department in default.

352. To complete the tabulation the accounts of Cash and

Merchandise (or the basic accounts, whatever they are) must be transcribed into linear form, commencing with the old balances and ending with the new. The debit and credit entries will undergo a kind of reversal: in the Cash account the receipts will be entered below the payments in column 3, the payments under the receipts in column 8; the purchases under the sales in column 4, the sales under the purchases in column 9. But the line of Cash and that of Merchandise will be in balance and the entire ledger will be tabulated. The columns will then correspond in pairs, as follows:

The totals will be equal, of columns 2 and 7.
3 and 8.
4 and 9.
5 and 10.
6 and 11.

Columns 2 and 7 having been compared with the totals of the old trial balance, so that nothing may be omitted, columns 6 and 11 will constitute the new trial balance.

353. It has even been thought worth while, in case the trial balance is taken at long intervals, to go first through the operation of tabulating instead of starting with the simple trial balance, columns 6 and 11 constituting the complete and only proof of accuracy. This is a laborious, but very thorough and satisfactory mode of proof.

CHAPTER XXI

FIDUCIARY ACCOUNTS

354. In the foregoing chapters, the accountancy was that of proprietorship, either sole or joint. The accounts were of two classes, constantly offsetting each other: accounts representing the proprietor in his relations with the outside world, and accounts representing things owned by him and persons in relation with him.

355. There is another class of accounts in which this idea of proprietorship is nearly or entirely absent, and its place is taken by responsibility or accountability. It always arises from delegated authority, the affairs being placed under the control of some person as representative of the actual owner whose object in keeping accounts is to prove that he has faithfully administered them.

356. The one who administers affairs which are not his own is variously named according to the nature of his functions or the source of his appointment. The *trustee* conducts the affairs of a *cestui-que-trust* or *beneficiary;* the *administrator*, or (if appointed by will) the *executor*, manages the *estate* of the *decedent*, who is either *intestate* or a *testator;* the *guardian* has charge of the affairs of a *ward;* the *committee* in lunacy, of those of an *incompetent;* the *comptroller* of a city, its financial affairs; a *receiver* is appointed for a *bankrupt;* an *assignee* for an *insolvent;* the

treasurer of a society or hospital or college accounts for its property, and its revenue and disbursements; a private person may confide his affairs to an *agent, attorney-in-fact, bailiff*, or *steward*. These terms are not uniformly used, there being many local variations. In all these cases the legal ownership is in the trustee, but the equitable ownership in those whom he represents.

357. The essence of fiduciary accounting is the ascertaining to what extent the person holding these delegated powers has fulfilled his duties and to what extent he is still accountable. He is *charged* with all property coming under his control, and he is *discharged* by any lawful disposal of it for the good of the estate.

358. An Estate account shows the extent of the accountability with which he is burdened at any time and this is a credit account corresponding to the proprietary account in commercial bookkeeping. It is not necessarily a measure of the wealth of the real proprietor but only of that which has come into the hands of the administrator of the trust and has not been duly disposed of.

359. What would be assets of the proprietor are charges against the administrator; but he may sometimes incur liabilities for which the estate is holden and if he satisfies these, or those to which the estate was subject, he is entitled to discharge thereby.

360. The functions of a *fiduciary* (by which term I describe generically any of the above representatives) may be considered under five heads:

1. Liquidation, or the reduction to a distributable form of the assets, and payments of the liabilities.
2. Collection of income.
3. Distribution of principal or income, or both, to whom it may concern.
4. Reinvestment.
5. Business management.

The executor or administrator is primarily a liquidator. His duty is to convert the assets into cash, to extinguish the liabilities, and to distribute the estate, performing the first and third functions.   Incidentally, he performs the second in the meantime.   With the fourth and fifth he is not ordinarily concerned. The testator, however, may have directed in his will that the estate be not all distributed forthwith, but certain property or certain sums are to be retained by a trusteee who is frequently the same person as the executor.   The trustee has as his duties the second and third functions, often the fourth.

361. When the fifth function is predominant, the accounts are indistinguishable from those of proprietary concerns; the struggle is for the attainment of wealth by the use of capital and the fiduciary departs from his proper functions as liquidator, collector, and distributor.   The "estate" then stands in the light of the capitalist and the fiduciary idea is eclipsed.   But as we recede from this to the original idea of a trust, the point of view is changed and the equation becomes:

$$\text{What I am charged with} = \text{what I can show as discharged} + \text{the net estate for which I am accountable}$$

362. The transactions of a fiduciary are analogous to those of a proprietary concern, but looked at inversely.   The ego is not the estate, but the trustee.   The two correlative sets of accounts spoken of in Article 354 exist, but it is the debits of the trustee against the credits of the estate, instead of the debits of the outsiders against the credits of the proprietor.   Yet if we take a transaction and analyze it after the manner of Chapter IV, we find that it falls into the same debits and credits whether the equation of proprietorship or that of accountability be followed. An increase of assets or an increased charge by reason of these assets are one and the same things as recorded.   It is not necessary therefore to burden the mind with any new rules for the record of transactions.

363. In strictly fiduciary accounting the economic accounts are minimized and there is no economic summary, as that is a

creature of business management. There is usually, for legal reasons, a very severe division between the principal of the estate and its income, and the latter is not thrown periodically into the former, but held in a separate credit balance, there being in this event two accounts:

THE ESTATE OF —————————, PRINCIPAL
THE ESTATE OF —————————, INCOME

364. Instead of a balance sheet, the fiduciary presents a report or accounting to the authority which conferred his powers upon him and this is by the custom of the courts composed in the form of "the trustee in account with the estate" and not the converse, the fiduciary stating first the sums with which he is chargeable and then what he claims in the way of discharge. Excellent models of such statements of account are given in *Hardcastle on the Accounts of Executors, etc.*, and more recently by John R. Loomis in *The Journal of Accountancy*, January, 1907.

365. A fact which will strike the commercial bookkeeper upon examining an executor's account is that the inventory with which it begins is an inventory of assets only, no reference being made to indebtedness even if shown on the books of the decedent, and no deduction being made for them. Debts only appear through their payment.

366. The account may be best made up from the estate account by reversal; that is, the fiduciary charges himself for amounts credited the estate and vice versa; this being preferable to making up the statement from the other accounts because mere permutations would have to be eliminated. The accounts should be kept with constant reference to the statement to be made to the court; and it is very desirable that each schedule should be represented by an account in the books of the fiduciary; the name of the schedule may form part of its title; as for example:

Schedule A
Increase on Appraised Value

Any asset being sold at an increased price, and the account representing it having been credited by cash received, the excess would be charged to the asset account and credited (not directly to the estate but) to Schedule A account. At the time of accounting Schedule A would be closed into Estate account in one sum.

367. It may be useful to illustrate the transformation of an Estate account into an accounting by an executor, who substitutes charges against himself for credits to the estate and vice versa. It is supposed that accounts have been opened as follows:

1. Estate of D. C. Dent.
2. Inventory.
3. Schedule A; increase on appraised value.
4. Schedule B; assets not in inventory.
5. Schedule C; income.
6. Schedule D; decrease on appraised value.
7. Schedule E; funeral charges and testamentary expenses.
8. Schedule F; debts and claims.
9. Schedule G; payments to widow.
10. Schedule H; expenses of administration.
11. Cash.

The accounts begin with the one entry:

Inventory/Estate

As the cash balance is included in the inventory, and as it is necessary to record the process of liquidation, the cash balance must be transferred to a separate account:

Cash/Inventory

The two accounts, Cash and Inventory, represent the executor and all the others represent the estate.

368. The executor then performs the following functions, and records them by the respective formulas:

Realization of assets in inventory:

Cash/Inventory

When such assets bring more than the inventoried value:

Inventory/Schedule A

When such assets bring less than the inventoried value:

Schedule D/Inventory

Realization of assets not in inventory:

Cash/Schedule B

Collection of income:

Cash/Schedule C

Necessary payments:

Schedule E, F, G, or H/Cash

369. At the time of balancing, all the other accounts are closed into the Estate account. It would be advisable to carry in the balances of Cash and Inventory in red ink, as they are the only balances which are to be carried forward to the next accounting.

FIGURE 55

ESTATE OF D. C. DENT

Schedule D.............	$ 600	Inventory..............		$43,000
" E.............	1,200	Schedule A.............		2,000
" F.............	8,300	" B.............		1,500
" G.............	2,400	" C.............		300
" H.............	2,150			
Inventory.............	*6,000*			
Cash.................	*26,150*			
	$46,800			$46,800

The arrangement of schedules is here precisely the same as that employed by Mr. Loomis in the paper cited in Article 364. I have not constituted an account for Schedule J, being "items in inventory uncollected," for the reason that I think these are better obtainable from the Inventory account itself.

The following would be the same account translated into the form of a surrogate's account, following the summary given by Mr. Loomis:

SUMMARY

I charge myself

With amount of Inventory................	$43,000	
" " " Schedule A..............	2,000	
" " " " B..............	1,500	
" " " " C..............	300	
Total Charges.................................		$46,800

I credit myself

With amount of Schedule D..............	$ 600	
" " " " E..............	1,200	
" " " " F..............	8,300	
" " " " G..............	2,400	
" " " " H..............	2,150	
" " " " J..............	6,000	
Total Credits.................................		20,650
Leaving a Balance of........................		$26,150

By comparing this with Figure 55 it will be seen that the charges of the accounting are made up from the credit of the Estate account and the credits of the accounting from the debit side of the Estate account.

370. It is not necessary to go as far into the details of fiduciary bookkeeping as we have with that of proprietary bookkeeping, since most of the mechanism of the latter is applicable to the former, and those details are derivable from the excellent treatises of Hardcastle and Gottsberger.

371. It may be remarked that the accounts of a savings bank (of the eastern or mutual type) while usually treated on the proprietary basis are strictly speaking fiduciary. The legal corporation is the board of trustees, yet they have no equitable interest in the assets; they merely administer a trust. The depositor is merely a creditor to the amount of his cash deposits and such interest or dividends as have been allotted him by the board; he has no legal title to the surplus, but has an equitable title, with his fellow depositors, to it. The surplus is a trust fund, for the benefit of the depositors at the time being, but not divisible except upon liquidation.

372. The failure to distinguish between proprietary and fiduciary accounts has led to some errors, such as the creation of a fictitious intermediary, "The Business," referred to in Article 133.

MONOGRAPH A
THE CASH ACCOUNT

MONOGRAPH A

THE CASH ACCOUNT

373. "Cash" taken as a concrete noun signifies in accounts
that which is received and paid in settlement; the medium of
liquidation. This is a somewhat imperfect definition of something which varies in the extent of its meaning. Some would
restrict the term to the meaning of "money" alone, but even then
it is difficult to fix the limitations of money itself. Shall we con-
fine it to full legal-tender specie, or shall we include bank notes
and treasury notes, which are really certificates of indebtedness?
We find that those who endeavor to narrow the field of cash
down to that which can be handled are inconsistent in so doing.
They will consider the check of another as cash, although it
merely conveys the *power* to receive an amount from some bank,
not even constituting an assignment of the amount; while on the
other hand amounts due us by a bank which need no act to make
them ours are excluded. The best usage, I think, recognizes as
the subject of the Cash account everything which can, according
to business custom, be used without question to extinguish liabilities or to acquire assets; in short, to carry out contracts.
Whatever is acceptable on either side as the fulfilment of a contract calling for dollars (or pounds, francs, marks, etc.) is in a
business sense "cash." In its potentialities it is the most versa-

tile of assets, for it is the only one which has at command every existent form whatever of property or service.

374. The cash is usually separated into two parts: cash on hand, and cash on deposit. The former is sometimes called "office" cash and the latter subdivision is frequently styled: "balance in bank," or (in England) "cash at the banker's." The latter phrase has been recently criticized by eminent British authority for fear lest it should be thought that it indicated the presence at the bank of sufficient coin or other tangible money specifically segregated and belonging to the account. But these fears are groundless; no one would make such a foolish mistake.

375. In modern times, cash "on hand" or in physical possession is overshadowed by bank cash, so that the payment of cash calls up the idea of writing checks rather than that of counting out money. The latter process is used only for the very insignificant dealings, and is sometimes designated as "petty cash."

376. There is a sense in which the Petty Cash account is sometimes kept which I cannot help considering as improper and dangerous. It is when the money transferred to Petty Cash is considered as expended, as far as the regular books are concerned, Petty Cash becoming a sort of economic account, equivalent to "minor expenses." There is supposed to be a book in which the keeper of the petty cash records the expenditures, but as he calls for round sums whenever his appropriation is nearly exhausted there is nothing in the system which makes a verification of his record compulsory. A much better plan, the imprest system, will be explained hereafter.

377. There is almost invariably a book called the "cash book," which contains in detail all the transactions affecting the cash, sometimes with other information. The relation of this book to the ledger is subject to the following variations:

1. There is a Cash account in the ledger, practically a summary of the cash book in weekly or monthly aggregates derived either from the journal or from the totals of the cash book.

2. The cash book is itself the Cash account, just as if it were a part of the ledger placed for convenience in a separate binding.

378. The scope of the cash book as to containing more or less branches of the cash gives rise to other variations.

1. The balance of the cash book may be considered as consisting of cash on hand, alone. All bank transactions are treated separately through a bank account or accounts.

(a) Deposits are usually treated as received into the office cash and then paid over to the bank, even when they consist of items which must eventually be deposited.

(b) Checks are treated in one of two ways:

(1) They are entered on both sides, as if the money were drawn from the bank and then paid over.

(2) They may appear in the bank account only, debited to the payee and credited to the bank.

2. The balance of the cash book may be considered as embracing both cash on hand and that on deposit. No distinction is made in the money columns between sums paid by check and those paid from cash on hand; nor between receipts remaining on hand and those deposited in bank, although such distinction may easily be indicated in the text. At each occasion of balancing the cash, however, the components must be separately stated: so much in bank, so much on hand, total so much.

3. By double columns on each side the cash on hand and that in bank are kept in the same book and yet distinct. Cross entries affecting both columns represent transfers between the bank and the office. This would appear from the text books to be the favorite method in Great Britain.

4. By the *imprest* system all transactions are forced ultimately to pass through the bank. The imprest is a fixed sum, usually an even amount, which is held in the office for the payment of petty purchases. There may be several imprests in the hands of various subordinates. When any payment is made

from the imprest cash, the bill, receipt, or voucher is counted temporarily as cash on hand, thus keeping the balance intact. If the imprest consists of $100, this may be $77 of it in payments made and receipted for and $23 in actual money. But from time to time the imprest must be replenished and always from the bank, a check being drawn for the entire $77 exactly and entered to the debit of the appropriate accounts; the check is cashed and the proceeds placed in the imprest. By making all other payments by check and by depositing all cash received, without exception, the cash transactions are faithfully represented by the bank account, and the cash balance at any time is the bank balance plus the fixed imprest. In this way the Cash account is checked from an independent source, the books of the bank.

379. The bank account to which the Cash account is now reduced is sometimes kept in the ledger, but the most detailed account is always contained in what is known as the "stub" of the check book. And there is no reason why, if this stub account is carefully kept, it should not supersede the bank account altogether.

380. Instead of a wide stub from which the checks are torn, an interleaved check book may be used, a leaf of checks between two pages which contain the account of checks and deposits. In keeping this account, the totals should be carried forward from page to page, not balanced at the foot of the page as is frequently done where the contents of the check book are to be transcribed into a cash book.

381. The Cash account is thus superseded by the check book record, which would have to be kept anyhow, and the procedure is greatly simplified. The old way was to copy the contents of the check book, together with the transactions of the office cash into a cash book; then to journalize this cash book, repeating all its contents; then to post from the journal to the ledger, which includes a Cash account as the fourth version of the same history.

382. Fiduciary accounts (Chapter XXI) lend themselves particularly well to this plan of making the check book into a complete cash book. Trust funds should always be kept separate from individual cash, and the proper way is for the fiduciary to open a bank account for and in the name of each trust which he may assume. His check book, suitably kept, will serve as the chief, or the only, book of account and posting medium. By the use of side posting (Article 271) he may minimize the labor of posting to a ledger or may dispense with it altogether if his accountability is solely for cash as, for example, the treasurership of a society; classification of receipts and expenditure being the only aim.

383. This plan of making the check book the medium of all transactions will not, for various reasons, be always practicable. When there are several bank accounts and several cashiers, it will often be simpler to unite their results in what may be called a "complex" cash book. This may be in the columnar form and the columnization may be on either of two principles: the one dividing the receipts and payments according to the *branch* of the cash to which they relate, the other according to the contra accounts involved in the transactions, the accounts credited when Cash is debited, and debited when Cash is credited; credited "by Cash" and debited "to Cash."

On the former plan, there will naturally be a pair of columns for each bank and a pair of columns for each cash-keeper and also a pair of columns for "the public." These last columns record those transactions which increase or decrease the total cash balance, as distinguished from those which are transfers between branches or receptacles. The public columns exactly correspond to the entries of Mode 2. Each transaction must necessarily, in this plan, enter into two columns, possibly into more. If it is an interior transaction, a shifting between departments, there must be a receipt in one and a payment in another. If it is an actual receipt or payment, from or to the outside world, it must affect the Public column and also some department.

384. The arrangement of these columns may be somewhat as follows:

FIGURE 56

RECEIVED							PAID				
From Teller A	From Teller B	From C Bank	From D Bank	From the Public			To the Public	To D Bank	To C Bank	To Teller B	To Teller A

Or perhaps these headings would be preferable:

Disbursed by Tellers		Drawn from Banks		Received from the Public	Parti-culars	Paid to the Public	Check List	Deposited in Banks		Received by Tellers	
Mr. A	Mr. B	C Natl.	D Natl.					D Natl.	C Natl.	Mr. B	Mr. A

The Check List column is a convenience for summing up the items received and to be deposited.

385. The second mode of columnization does not concern itself with the components of the cash, but with the consideration which caused it to change hands, the equivalents which were received and given; the wherefore, not the where. This is done for the purpose of forming totals which may be posted in mass, usually monthly, or, following the old conceptions, to make the cash book self-journalizing.

386. Both kinds of cash book may be kept concurrently in an extensive business, where all cash transactions have their origin in tickets or vouchers. They will usually, then, be a daily cash book of the first columnar plan and a monthly cash book of the second, the former being balanced every day and the latter at the end of each month.

387. The monthly, or journalized cash book, as well as the simple form 2, admit of columnizing some values which are not receipts nor payments, but are *concomitants* of those transactions; and thus the keeping of a special posting medium is avoided. As an example of this, we may take the subject of *cash discounts*.

388. Indebtedness for purchases is usually subject to a stipulation that the purchaser may settle at an earlier time than is required by the contract and in consideration of such prepayment shall be entitled to a discount stated in a percentage of the full, or gross, price. Thus it happens that many, or most, of the cash amounts paid or received in settlement of such indebtedness are less than the amount standing on the account as due; and that it cannot be determined until the payment is actually made whether the discount option will be utilized, or at what rate. In case of a debtor the settlement will be:

$$\left.\begin{array}{l} \text{Cash} \\ \text{Discount} \end{array}\right\} \; /\text{Customer}$$

The discount is a concomitant of the cash entry and it will evidently be an advantage if the entries can be made concurrently without having to repeat the particulars. For this purpose two additional columns are provided, one for the gross amount of the bill, one for the amount of the discount, and the third for the actual cash received.

CUSTOMERS

Gross	Discount	Cash	
$2,934.62	$58.69	$2,875.93	

The third column only is used for balancing the cash. The middle column in total is posted at the end of the month to the debit of Discount, an economic account, the aggregate of which at the balancing period should be carried to the debit of Sales, or of the Trading account. The first column is equal to the sum of the other two if the subtractions of the discount have been correctly made and this test should always be applied.

389. As to posting to the customer's account the simplest way is post the gross amount without distinguishing between cash and discount. It might be thought best to state these separately, in order to leave a record of whether the customer pays promptly or foregoes discount; but if this is not sufficiently indicated by the date, a memorandum of the rate of discount may be inserted in the posting; as:

$$\text{Apr. 5 } (-\ 2\%),\ \$2,934.62$$

which would be far more expressive than:

$$\text{Apr. 5 By Cash, } \$2,934.62$$

390. Another way of entering the discount without a concomitant column is to represent that the entire amount has been received and the discount refunded:

Received from Customer................	$2,934.62
Expended for Discount.................	$58.69

This follows the fact less closely than the method by concomitant column, and it does not agree with the bank pass book, which will record only $2,875.93 as deposited.

This latter, more fictitious method by two cash entries is often used for discounting bills receivable, but even there I think the concomitant method will frequently be found preferable.

391. In Article 275 a device was explained by which the cash book is made to perform the work of the journal by introducing two equal and opposite amounts. This would be objectionable in a check book used as cash book, for it would break up the correspondence between the account kept by the bank and that kept by the depositor. Nevertheless the shifting of debits and credits may be effected by drawing a check to your *own* order, and, instead of issuing it, depositing it to your own credit. For example, A is a customer who, besides buying of you, occasionally sells you some special article. As you prefer to keep your personal debtors and creditors separate, you have two accounts with A, one in each capacity. He owes you $270 on the one account and you owe him $30 on the other. He sends you the net amount $240, instead of sending $270 and waiting for you to return $30. To avoid a journal entry transferring the $30 from one account to the other, you draw a check for the $30 not to his order but to your own, since he has already paid himself; this check you charge to him, but deposit it along with the $240, making up the $270 necessary to balance his account as a customer.

392. The reduction of the cash book, the Cash account, and the bank account to the one form of the check book is a great simplification, but it has been found that the check book itself may be simplified. What is known as the check register is beginning to supplant it. Instead of containing only three, or at most six checks to a page, thirty to fifty may be described on a page, provided we utterly abandon the idea of a stub from which the check is torn and enter the descriptive matter on a single line. The checks are made up in pads and are numbered in advance, as are also the lines of the register. The rule must be inflexible that the entry on the register shall be made *first* and the check filled out from it; in fact, this ought to be the rule when the stub is used, for a check might be issued without record. The vacant stub is somewhat more of a reminder than the numbered line, yet it is thought better to forego this advantage rather than to lose so much time in adding up every four or five checks.

This plan is mostly used by banks issuing drafts which are practically checks on other banks, and is then called a "draft register." Its introduction is facilitated by the fact that no contra account of deposits needs to be kept on the same page.

Without the invention of blocks or pads of blanks, which keep the papers firmly in their proper order, this form of register would have been impracticable.

393. I propose a new method of handling the cash transactions, or rather a recurrence to the original plan of a ledger account, with the aid of the following comparatively modern devices: pads of blanks; machine numbering; cards or loose leaves for accounts; ticket posting, and perhaps carbon-duplication.

There should be a memorandum blank of the same size as the check and bearing the same number, on which should be entered all the data of the check necessary to make it a posting ticket.

FIGURE 57

MEMORANDUM OF CHECK

Check No. *5693* on First National Bank

$500.   *July 15, 1907*

Payable to *William Jones*

Charge to   *do*

CHECK

No. 5693   New York, *July 15, 1907*

FIRST NATIONAL BANK

Pay to the order of *William Jones*_____

*Five hundred*_____Dollars

$500.   *John Smith*

The tickets and the checks should alternate in the same pad, the ticket always *above* its check, so that it would be impossible to "forget" to make the entry, and this plan would be at least as effective as the stub.

394. The bank account would be kept as part of the ledger on its own card or its own leaves. The check memorandum would be posted to the credit of the account and likewise to the debit of some other account and then filed.

395. This method is not always applicable, as there are certain circumstances which seem to demand the existence of a check book; but it seems to me to be very nearly the ultimatum of directness and simplicity.

396. A modification, using carbon duplication, may be used when numerous checks are drawn in succession and the typewriter is used for filling them in. The checks will be on a long strip with perforations between (instead of being padded) and a similar strip will be behind it with the carbon between. This strip, taking the place of the memorandum tickets, gives a facsimile of all the filling. It may or may not have printed matter so as to interpret its contents.

This plan has been used with great success for pay-roll checks drawn on a bank which is used for this sole purpose and where a deposit is made of the exact total of each set of checks, which total is obtained by adding the carbon strip. In this case, the strips are not torn off and used as posting tickets, since no individual accounts need to be kept with the payee; the total is posted in bulk to the Labor account.

397. In whatever form the account of cash is kept, its verification, or "balancing the cash," cannot be neglected. Cash on hand should invariably be verified daily, because the difficulty of tracing an error increases with the lapse of time. With cash on deposit, which is less liquid, the error is generally in calculation only, and a daily proof, though not so necessary as in cash on hand, is still desirable.

398. It is unnecessary, and generally undesirable, to break the columns of a Cash account by the insertion and carrying forward of a balance. A memorandum in the margin, showing that the difference between the two totals is exactly accounted for by the values found, is just as effective for this purpose and the totals themselves generally have a certain utility.

399. The bank account as exhibited in the check book should be made to tally with that rendered by the bank itself in the pass book or the monthly statement. This is a most valuable corroboration as it is furnished by a person outside of the concern. Hence in any suspected case of fraud, and even in any ordinary case, the accountant will seize upon the pass book and check book as among the most valuable bases for his examination.

400. In case of audit, it has been claimed by some that the verification of the cash balance is no part of the duty of the auditor. From a practical standpoint, I should be disposed to question this dictum, and an actual instance may be adduced to the contrary. A trust company, as receiver of a hotel, employed a cashier and general bookkeeper, dishonest and afterwards a convict. The trust company retained a firm of public accountants to make a monthly audit of the accounts, which they did, and passed them as correct. The actual cash balance, however, was very different from that shown in the books, which was fictitious. The cash on hand consisted, in addition to the real money needed, of a large amount of memorandums, worthless checks, etc. This would have made the balance on hand appear absurdly large, but the embezzler, to conceal this, overdrew the bank account constantly, but held back, unissued, checks to dealers in supplies, which had been regularly signed, and the amount charged to the dealers' accounts. The cash balance of,

say..	$10,000
was composed of worthless paper..................	$40,000
less overdraft at bank...........................	30,000
	$10,000

The auditors paid no attention to this on the ground that it was not their duty to verify the cash balance. How they could neglect the balance of the check book does not appear, for it was the posting medium for the dealers ledger. They contented themselves with the nominal net balance, without inquiring into its components; they do not appear to have even inquired why the bookkeeper did not fill out a printed form appearing at the end of each month in the general cash book which called for a detailed statement of the items composing the cash. It seems to me that an audit which does not probe the bank account is almost worthless.*

401. In the verification of the bank balance, it seldom happens that the same result is shown in our account and in the account rendered by the bank. The cause of this is that, as in other accounts of indebtedness, there is an interval of time between the payment on the one hand and the receipt on the other, so that the transaction is for a time in transit, and necessarily appears under one date in one account and under another in the other. Where deposits are made by mail, this is often the case. Where checks are issued, they do not ordinarily reach the bank on the same day and frequently are "outstanding" for many days. It is therefore necessary to make a reconciliation between the two balances and this should be made a permanent record, so as to facilitate the next following reconciliation.

402. I would recommend that the balance of *our* account be first brought down and made the basis of the reconciliation, a total of the checks being inserted above the balance, as in Figure 11. Next the deposit side is examined. This is composed of the previous balance which was adjusted and the deposits since made. If these are all in, the totals of the left-hand side should agree. Next, the checks actually canceled and returned should

---

* I have no intention to assert, nor do I believe, that any such view is usual among American certified public accountants; but I am emphasizing the point that this is poor auditing. Possibly the contract for auditing expressly excluded verification of cash; in that case the trust company was to blame.

be compared with the list accompanying them, after which they should be reassorted by serial numbers into the order in which they were originally drawn. A list of the missing checks should then be made up. The total of this list should exactly equal the difference between the two aggregates of checks, as drawn and as paid.

Having thus reconciled each side of the account, we are prepared to record the results. The general principle to be followed is that we must bring the balance on our books into conformity with the bank's statement for a moment, so that in the next reconciliation, if there is no variance, one side will be identical. If the variance is caused by delay only, and not by actual error on either side, we restore our account to its original status.

403. Suppose that there are 5 deposits and 5 checks, giving on our books the following result:

Deposits		Checks	
$633.34	No. 1	$200.00	
522.19	2	400.00	
300.00	3	199.73	
456.97	4	108.00	
250.00	5	329.14	
	Total.....	$1,236.87	....
	Balance....	925.63	
$2,162.50		$2,162.50	

Balance..... $925.63

If all the deposits have reached the bank and all the checks have been paid, the figures $2,162.50, $1,236.87, and $925.63 will coincide and no adjustment will be necessary. But we will now suppose that checks No. 2 and No. 4 are outstanding; also that the last deposit, $250, had not yet been credited by the bank; therefore the balance as rendered by the bank is $1,183.63, the difference between $1,912.50 and $728.87. The checks outstanding are re-entered on *both* sides of our account; the deposit in transit is subtracted from the balance, which then agrees on the debit side with the bank statement; but the deposit, as it will reach the bank before the next reconciliation, is restored to its place.

		Total...................	$1,236.87
		Balance...............	925.63
	$2,162.50		$2,162.50

Balance............	$925.63		
+ Checks outstanding...	508.00		
	$1,433.63		
— Deposit in transit.....	250.00		
Balance as per pass book	$1,183.63	No. 2...................	$400.00
Deposit in transit...	250.00	No. 4...................	108.00

404. An audit involving checks outstanding can only be regarded as provisional and is not complete until those checks have been paid and their amounts re-examined.

405. One of the most important points to be considered in the inauguration of a system of accounts is the method of handling the cash and its record in the Cash account, whether kept in the ledger, in a cash book, or in a check book.

MONOGRAPH B
THE MERCHANDISE ACCOUNT

MONOGRAPH B

THE MERCHANDISE ACCOUNT

406. The reader has been cautioned (Article 200) against mixed accounts; that is, accounts partly specific and partly economic. These will, however, sometimes occur through the imperfections of current accounting: an account which is normally economic will prove to have a residue of the specific when it comes to the nicer adjustment of the balance sheet, and vice versa. This has been touched upon in the cases of Coal (Articles 174–181) and Interest (Articles 185–194).

407. There are accounts, as sometimes kept, where it cannot be said that either the specific or economic character predominates, where each phase is important and essential, and where, if practicable, the course of wisdom would be to create two accounts, one representing the specific and the other the economic side of the transactions.

408. A good example of such an account is the Merchandise account in the form still prevalent but gradually falling into disuse. It is not recommended for adoption, but its structure should be understood, in order that, when encountered in the course of examination of accounts, it may be readily disentangled.

409. Merchandise is something bought at a certain cost price for the purpose of selling at a higher price. The latter price consists of two parts—one equal to the cost, which it repays, the other the merchandise profit, which is earned by services in bringing the goods near the customer, in selecting them with reference to their desirable qualities, in providing a convenient place where they may be inspected, and in holding enough in stock to meet all reasonable demands.

410. Viewed in this light, every sale is properly creditable to two accounts, one part to the asset, merchandise parted with, the other to the Income account for the profit.

411. But it seems to be considered in retail business, even on a large scale, impracticable to separate each sale into its two elements, and to know at each transaction how much goes to replace the goods, and how much to repay the merchant for services, risk, and expense. One would suppose it feasible, and some merchants find it so, to record in a column of the sales book the original cost of each article. But more usually the sale price is undivided.

412. The Merchandise account, therefore, becomes a mixed account. On the debit side, it contains entries at cost price, and on the credit side at selling price. No correlation is revealed between the two sets of values, any more than if one were in rupees and the other in reichsmarks.

Hence some writers, in their zeal for classification, have considered the Merchandise account as purely an outlay and income account. The merchandise is considered, not as property but rather as a mere form of cash expenditure to be recouped ultimately by receipts of a greater amount, the resultant being profit. A difficulty arises when we reflect that the merchandise on hand *is* property of too great value to be ignored. The way to get over this difficulty is to consider the merchandise on hand as an adjustment—an offset to the purchases.

413. Other authors again would classify this account as strictly a specific account—an asset. The difficulty here is that if we attempt to balance such an account we get a meaningless balance, corresponding to nothing. Hence the assumption is made that there is an increment of value to the extent of the profit; that the merchandise, so far as sold, has appreciated to that extent.

414. But whether the Merchandise account be regarded as specific, or economic, or, as I contend, mixed, the calculation and the recording of the result are substantially the same. Let us take as an example, the following facts:

Merchandise on hand January 1.............	$5,643.75
Bought during January....................	2,644.18
Sold during January......................	3,219.74
Bought during February..................	1,845.17
Sold during February.....................	2,454.62
Bought during March.....................	1,929.44
Sold during March.......................	1,728.96

From these data let us construct an account:

FIGURE 58

MERCHANDISE

Jan.	1	Balance........	$5,643.75				
"		Purchases......	2,644.18	Jan.		Sales.........	$3,219.74
Feb.		"	1,845.17	Feb.		"	2,454.62
Mar.		"	1,929.44	Mar.		"	1,728.96

But from this we can draw no conclusion. The debit side amounts to $12,062.54 and the credit side to $7,403.32, but the difference, $4,659.22, is not an asset, for that would be assuming that we have sold at cost price; and it cannot be a loss, for that would be assuming that there is no balance remaining. If we know the profit, we can ascertain the balance; if we know the balance, we can ascertain the profit.

415. The balance on hand, ascertained by inventory, is the key to the situation. Assume that it is $6,894.16. Then we compute the profit thus:

Merchandise on hand January 1..........................		$5,643.75
Bought in January............................	$2,644.18	
" February............................	1,845.17	
" March................................	1,929.44	
Total bought..		6,418.79
Total cost..		$12,062.54
But there remains *un*sold at cost..........................		6,894.16
Therefore the goods sold must have cost...................		$5,168.38

But they produced:

in January..................................... $3,219.74
February.................................. 2,454.62
March..................................... 1,728.96

Total proceeds...................................... 7,403.32

and the profit must be.................................. $2,234.94

416. We can now complete our account.

FIGURE 59

MERCHANDISE

Jan. 1	Balance (inv.).	$5,643.75			
Jan.	Purchases.....	2,644.18	Jan.	Sales........	$3,219.74
Feb.	"	1,845.17	Feb.	"	2,454.62
Mar.	"	1,929.44	Mar.	"	1,728.96
	Profit........	*2,234.94*		*Balance (Inv.)*	*6,894.16*
		$14,297.48			$14,297.48

$6,894.16 goes to the balance sheet; $2,234.94 to the Profit and Loss account.

417. This is the traditional form of the Merchandise account and suffices perfectly for "balancing the books." Its defect is that it nowhere presents a clearly contrasted statement of the same goods at the two prices—in and out—and consequently the average percentage of profit could not be obtained without effort.

418. When there are goods returned, whether purchases returned by us or sales returned to us, the confusion is still greater, for each side contains some values at cost price and some at selling price. To illustrate this, let us vary the above figures slightly, the final results being the same:

Balance January 1, as per Inventory.............. $5,643.75
We purchased in January....................... 2,760.18
but returned............................... 116.00
We sold in January........................... 3,452.74
but had returned........................... 233.00
We purchased in February...................... 1,865.17
but returned..... · · 20.00

We sold in February...............................	2,937.62
but had returned..............................	483.00
We purchased in March..........................	1,947.44
but returned.................................	18.00
We sold in March..............................	1,903.96
but had returned..............................	175.00
Balance March 31, as per inventory..............	6,894.16

419. It will be readily seen that the difficulty of obtaining intelligible information as to the comparative values, in and out, is even greater than in Figure 59, and that to obtain such information the account would need to be taken to pieces and made over:

FIGURE 60

MERCHANDISE

Jan.	1	Balance......	$5,643.75				
"		Purchases....	2,760.18	Jan.		Returns......	$116.00
"		Returns......	233.00	"		Sales........	3,452.74
Feb.		Purchases....	1,865.17	Feb.		Returns......	20.00
"		Returns......	483.00	"		Sales........	2,937.62
Mar.		Purchases	1,947.44	Mar.		Returns......	18.00
"		Returns......	175.00	"		Sales........	1,903.96
"	31	*Profit*........	*2,234.94*	"	31	*Balance......*	*6,894.16*
			$15,342.48				$15,342.48

420. *An account which needs to be made over is one which ought to have been made differently at first.*

421. The modern practice is to separate the Merchandise account into three: Merchandise, Sales, and Purchases; or at least the former two.

The above transactions would be posted as follows:

FIGURE 61

MERCHANDISE

Jan.	1	Balance........	$5,643.75	

PURCHASES

Jan. Total bought......	$2,760.18	Jan. Total returned by us	$116.00
Feb. " "	1,865.17	Feb. " " " "	20.00
Mar. " "	1,947.44	Mar. " " " "	18.00

SALES

Jan. Total returned to us	$233.00	Jan. Total sold.........	$3,452.74
Feb. " " " "	483.00	Feb. " "	2,937.62
Mar. " " " "	175.00	Mar. " "	1,903.96

Next close Purchases into Merchandise:

PURCHASES

Jan. Total bought......	$2,760.18	Jan. Total returned by us	$116.00
Feb. " "	1,865.17	Feb. " " " "	20.00
Mar. " "	1,947.44	Mar. " " " "	18.00
			$154.00
		Net Purchases.....	*6,418.79*
	$6,572.79		$6,572.79

MERCHANDISE

Jan. Balance.....	$5,643.75
Jan.-Mar. Purchases....	6,418.79
	$12,062.54

In Sales account bring down the balance:

SALES

Jan. Total returned to us	$233.00	Jan. Total sold.........	$3,452.74
Feb. " " " "	483.00	Feb. " "	2,937.62
Mar. " " " "	175.00	Mar. " "	1,903.96
	$891.00		
Carried down.....	*7,403.32*		
	$8,294.32		$8,294.32
		Net Sales.....	$7,403.32

422. The cost of goods sold is now obtained by subtracting from the total of:

Merchandise...	$12,062.54
the present balance......................................	6,894.16
cost of goods sold..	$5,168.38

423. The only two accounts remaining open are Merchandise and Sales.

Sales/Merchandise............................. $5,168.38

Having posted this entry, the Merchandise, a pure asset account, is closed into the balance sheet; the Sales account, a pure outlay and income account, shows the cost and the proceeds *of the same goods*, and the difference is carried to the economic summary.

FIGURE 62

MERCHANDISE

Jan. 1	Balance.....	$5,643.75			
Jan.-Mar.	Purchases...	6,418.79	Jan.-Mar. Sales, at cost.		$5,168.38
			Mar. 31	*Balance*.....	6,894.16
		$12,062.54			$12,062.54

SALES

Jan.-Mar.	Cost of goods		Jan.-Mar. Net proceeds...	$7,403.32
	sold......	$5,168.38		
	Profit.......	*2,234.94*		
		$7,403.32		$7,403.32

INDEX

185